A SHORT HISTORY OF THE AMERICAN NEGRO

REVISED EDITION

BY

BENJAMIN BRAWLEY

DEAN OF MOREHOUSE COLLEGE

AUTHOR OF "THE NEGRO IN LITERATURE AND ART," "YOUR
NEGRO NEIGHBOR," "AFRICA AND THE WAR," ETC.

ISBN: 978-1-63923-835-4

Printed: March 2023

Published and Distributed By:
Lushena Books
607 Country Club Drive, Unit E
Bensenville, IL 60106
www.lushenabks.com

ISBN: 978-1-63923-835-4

A SHORT HISTORY OF THE AMERICAN NEGRO

DEDICATED
ON THE FIFTIETH ANNIVERSARY
OF NEGRO EMANCIPATION
TO THE YOUNG AMERICANS
WITH WHOM IT HAS BEEN MY PRIVILEGE
IN THE CLASSROOM TO SEEK
THE BEAUTIFUL AND THE TRUE

PREFACE

This study of the history of the American Negro endeavors simply to set forth the main facts about the subject that one might wish to know, and to supply in some measure the historical background for much that one reads to-day in newspapers and magazines. The book presupposes only an elementary knowledge of American history, but it does presuppose so much. The principle has been adhered to throughout that institutions are greater than men; hence little chronicle of individual achievement has been attempted, individuals being mentioned generally only when they had to do with significant movements. From the nature of the discussion the treatment could hardly be primarily original, and frequent citation is made to the conclusions of investigators along special lines. At the same time it is hoped that in more than one instance the presentation will be found to be substantially new. It has been the aim to deal with different phases of the life of the Negro—political, economic, social, religious, cultural—with some degree of proportion; but because of the great importance of education since the Civil War, special attention may **not** unnaturally seem to be given to this feature. For a more intimate expression of some social phases of the subject than is here attempted, such books as Mr. Baker's "Following the Colour Line" and Dr. Washington's "The Story of the Negro" should be read.

It is perhaps only when one enters upon such a study as this that he realizes how valuable are the investigations of Dr. W. E. B. DuBois in this field. For the earlier years the thesis, "The Suppression of the African Slave-Trade," is really indispensable; and one of the chapters is largely based on the Atlanta University publication, "The Negro Church." In a similar way is another chapter based upon the valuable study by Dr. R. R. Wright, Jr., entitled "Self-Help in Negro Education." The last chapter is naturally much · indebted to my own publication, "The Negro in Literature and Art."

The composition of the book has been a pleasant task because of the sympathetic interest it has awakened. If I should here set down the names of all those who have assisted me by conversation, by letter, or otherwise, the list would be a long one. There are a few persons, however, to whom my thanks are more than ordinarily due; but no one whom I may mention is in any way responsible for any statement herein contained, unless he is directly quoted. Of the Department of History of the University of Chicago, Professor Shepardson has given me some valuable suggestions; Dr. Jernegan will recognize my indebtedness to him more than once; and Professor Dodd, with his accustomed generosity, has taken unusual time and pains in helping me to arrive at accurate conclusions. Mr. Henry E. Baker, of the United States Patent Office, the authority on the subject of Negro inventors, has helped me greatly in his special field. Mr. Emmett J. Scott, of Tuskegee Institute and more recently of the War Department, has kindly assisted on special points; while any student of the subject must now be indebted to the good work that is being done by the *Journal of Negro History.* For helpful criticism I feel grateful to my colleagues at Morehouse College and Howard University, while to my father, Rev. E. M. Brawley, I am indebted for aid so various and so freely given that space fails me either to record the instances or to enumerate the kinds.

Since the first edition of this book was issued in 1913 great and wonderful changes have taken place in the life of the Negro people of the United States. More than half a million of them have changed their place of work and residence, while four hundred thousand men have taken part in the greatest war in history. In sending forth the revised edition of the book I am reminded once more of the sense of co-operation that has come to me from teachers who have found the work useful as a text, and I wish them all joy as they further pursue their task of directing the youth of the race to noble ideals.

BENJAMIN BRAWLEY.

ATLANTA,
April 22, 1919.

CONTENTS

CHAPTER I

CHAPTER II

CHAPTER III

CHAPTER IV

CHAPTER V

CHAPTER XI

CHAPTER XII

CHAPTER XIII

CHAPTER XIV

A SHORT HISTORY OF THE AMERICAN NEGRO

CHAPTER I

BEGINNINGS OF SLAVERY IN THE COLONIES

1. The Word Negro.—The word *Negro* is the modern Spanish and Portuguese form of the Latin adjective *niger*, meaning *black*. As commonly used, the word is made to apply to any and all of the black and dark brown races of Africa. Such a usage is not strictly correct, the term having both a narrower and a wider significance than this would imply. In Africa the real Negroes occupy only a relatively small part of the continent, while outside of Africa, on the islands of the Pacific Ocean, there is a branch of the Nigritian race of people only less important than the main branch of Negroes in Africa.

2. African Slave Coast.—The Negroes who came to America as slaves were by no means all of exactly the same race stock and language. Plantations frequently exhibited a variety of customs, and sometimes traditional enemies became brothers in servitude. The center of the colonial slave-trade was the African coast for about two hundred miles east of the great Niger River. From this comparatively small region came as many slaves as from all the rest of Africa together. A number of those who came were of entirely different race stock from the Negroes; some were Moors, and a very few were Malays from Madagascar. Such wide differences in race and tribal origin account for the very marked distinctions of form and feature to be observed to-day in Americans of unmixed African descent.

3. The Negro in Spanish Exploration.—Negroes are mentioned in the very earliest accounts of explorers in America, even by Columbus in the records of his voyages. After 1501 they became familiar personages in the West Indies; and in 1513 thirty Negroes assisted Balboa in building the first ships made on the Pacific Coast of America. On his accession to the Spanish throne Charles V granted "license for the introduction [into America] of Negroes to the number of four hundred" (1517), and thereafter importation to the West Indies became a thriving industry. Those who came in these early years were sometimes men of considerable intelligence, having been trained as Mohammedans or Catholics. It was about 1525 that Negroes were first introduced within the present limits of the United States. These were brought to a colony near what is now Jamestown, Va. In course of time the Negroes here were so harshly treated that they rose in insurrection against their oppressors and fired their houses. The settlement was broken up, and the Negroes and their Spanish companions returned to Hayti, whence they had come. The best authenticated case cf a Negro's leading in exploration is that of Estevanico, or Estevanillo, one of the four survivors of the ill-fated expedition of De Narvaez, who sailed from Spain June 17, 1527. The three companions of this man returned to Spain; but he himself became a medicine-man among the natives, and later became highly esteemed by those interested in extending the Spanish domain. To him belongs the credit of the discovery of the Zuñi Indians and of New Mexico. No part played by the Negro in these early years, however, exercised any abiding influence on the history of the race in the United States.

4. Beginnings of the African Slave-Trade.—The revival of slavery at the close of the Middle Ages and the beginning of the system of Negro slavery were due to the commercial expansion of Portugal in the fifteenth century. In 1441 Prince Henry sent out one Gonzales, who captured three Moors on the African Coast. These offered as ransom ten Negroes whom they had taken. The Negroes were brought to Lisbon in 1442, and in 1444 Prince Henry regularly began the European trade from the Guinea Coast.

For fifty years his country enjoyed a monopoly of the traffic. The slaves were taken at first to Europe, and later to the Spanish possessions in America, where Indian slavery did not work well. Spain herself joined in the trade in 1517, and as early as 1530 William Hawkins, a merchant of Plymouth, visited the Guinea Coast and took away a few slaves. England really entered the field, however, with the voyage in 1562 of Captain John Hawkins, son of William, who also went to the west coast of Africa. Captain Hawkins made two other voyages, one in 1564 in the good ship *Jesus*, and another, with Drake, in 1567, taking his slaves to the West Indies. Queen Elizabeth evidently regarded the opening of the slave-trade as a worthy achievement, for when she made Hawkins a knight she gave him for a crest the device of a Negro's head and bust with the arms securely bound. France joined in the traffic in 1624, and then Holland, Denmark, and the American colonies.

5. **Development of the Slave-Trade by England.**—
The rivalry between the different countries of Europe over the slave-trade soon became intense; and England, with her usual aggressiveness, soon assumed a commanding position. "The commercial supremacy of the Dutch in the first part of the seventeenth century excited the envy and the emulation of the English. The Navigation Ordinance of 1651 was aimed

at them, and two wars were necessary to wrest the slave-trade from them and place it in the hands of the English." * The English trade proper began with the granting of rights to special companies, to one in 1618, to another in 1631, and in 1662 to the "Company of Royal Adventurers," rechartered in 1672 as the "Royal African Company." James, Duke of York, was interested in this last company, and it agreed in a contract to supply the West Indies with 3,000 slaves annually. In 1698, on account of the incessant clamor of English merchants, the commerce was opened generally, and private traders by act of parliament were allowed to participate in it on payment of a duty of 10 per cent. on English goods exported to Africa. The market for the slaves was the American colonies of the European countries, at first especially the Spanish West Indies. In course of time England came to regard the slave-trade as of such importance that when in 1713 she accepted the Peace of Utrecht she insisted on having awarded to her for thirty-three years the exclusive right to transport slaves to the Spanish colonies in America.

6. Planting of Slavery in the Colonies.—(a) Virginia. It is only for Virginia that we can state with definiteness the year in which Negro slaves were first brought to an English colony on the mainland. When

* DuBois, *Suppression of the Slave-Trade*, 17.

legislation on the subject of slavery first appears else-where, slaves are already present. In August, 1619, a Dutch vessel brought to Jamestown twenty Negroes,* who were sold into servitude. Virginia, however, did not give statutory recognition to slavery as a system until 1661, the importations being too small to make the matter one of importance. In this year, however, an act of assembly stated that Negroes were "in-capable of making satisfaction for the time lost in running away by addition of time; † and thus slavery gained a firm place in the oldest of the colonies.

(b) Massachusetts. Negroes were first imported into Massachusetts from Barbadoes a year or two before 1638, but in John Winthrop's Journal, under date February 26th of this year, we have positive evidence on the subject as follows: "Mr. Pierce in the Salem ship, the Desire, returned from the West Indies after seven months. He had been at Providence, and brought some cotton, and tobacco, and negroes, etc., from thence, and salt from Tertugos. Dry fish and strong liquors are the only commodities for those parts. He met there two men-of-war, sent forth by the lords, etc., of Providence with letters of mart, who had taken divers prizes from the spaniard and

---

* DuBois, *Suppression of the Slave-Trade,* 17.
† Hening, II, 26.

many negroes." It was in 1641 that there was passed in Massachusetts the first act on the subject of slavery; and this was the first positive act in any of the colonies with reference to the matter. It was enacted that "there shall never be any bond slavery, villeinage, nor captivity among us, unless it be lawful captives, taken in just wars, and such strangers as willingly sell themselves or are sold to us, and these shall have all the liberties and Christian usages which the law of God established in Israel requires." This article clearly sanctioned slavery. Of the three classes of persons referred to, the first was made up of Indians, the second of white people under the system of indenture (of which more must be said), and the third of Negroes. In this whole matter, as in many others, Massachusetts moved in advance of the other colonies. The first definitely to legalize slavery, she early became the foremost representative of the sentiment against the system. In these early years the New England colonies were more concerned about Indians than about Negroes, as the presence of the former in large numbers was a constant menace, while Negro slavery had not yet assumed its more serious aspects.

(c) New York. Slavery began in New York under the Dutch rule and continued under the English. Before or about 1650 the Dutch West India Company brought Negro slaves to New Netherland. Most of these continued to belong to the company, though after a period of labor (under the common system of indenture) some of the more trusty were allowed to have small farms, from the produce of which they made return to the company. Their children, however, continued to be slaves. In 1664 New Netherland became New York. The next year, in the code of English laws that was drawn up, it was enacted that "no Christian shall be kept in bond slavery, villeinage, or captivity, except who shall be judged thereunto by authority, or such as willingly have sold or shall sell themselves." As at first there was hesitancy about making Negroes Christians, this act, like the one in Massachusetts, by implication permitted slavery.

(d) Maryland. It was in 1632 that the grant including what is now the states of Maryland and Delaware was made to George Calvert, first Lord Baltimore. Though slaves are mentioned earlier, it was in 1663–4 that the Maryland legislature passed its first enactment on the subject of slavery. It was declared that "all negroes and other slaves within this province, and all negroes and other slaves to be hereinafter imported into this province, shall serve during life; and all children born of any negro or other slave, shall be slaves as their fathers were, for the term of their lives."

(e) Delaware and New Jersey. The real beginnings of slavery in these colonies are unusually hazy. The Dutch introduced the system in both New Jersey and Delaware. In the laws of New Jersey the word *slaves* occurs as early as 1664, and acts for the regulation of the conduct of those in bondage began with the practical union of the colony with New York in 1702. The lot of the slave was somewhat better here than in most of the colonies. Although the system was in existence in Delaware almost from the beginning of the colony, it did not receive legal recognition until 1721, when there was passed an act providing for the trial of slaves by two justices and six freeholders. Delaware was influenced a good deal in her views by Pennsylvania, the Quaker colony where slavery was generally opposed though tolerated.

(f) Pennsylvania. Especially in its earlier years, by reason of the sturdy and independent character of its settlers, the colony of Pennsylvania became noteworthy for its opposition to the enslavement of Negroes, and early acts on the subject were largely restrictive. When slavery is first heard of in Pennsylvania, in 1688, a memorial against the system is drawn up by Francis Daniel Pastorius for the Germantown Quakers. In 1700 the legislature forbade the selling of slaves out of the province without their consent, and the importation of slaves from Carolina was prohibited in 1705 on the ground that it made trouble with the Indians nearer home.

(g) Connecticut. It was almost by accident that slavery was officially recognized in Connecticut in 1650. The code of laws compiled for the colony in this year was especially harsh on the Indians. It was enacted that certain of them who incurred the displeasure of the colony might be made to serve a person injured by them or "be shipped out and exchanged for negroes." In 1680 the governor of the colony informed the Board of Trade that "as for blacks there came sometimes three or four in a year from Barbadoes, and they are usually sold at the rate of £22 apiece." These people were regarded rather as servants than as slaves, and early legislation was mainly in the line of police regulations designed to prevent their running away.

(h) Rhode Island. In 1652 it was enacted in Rhode Island that all slaves brought into the colony should be set free after ten years of service. This law was not designed, as might be supposed, to restrict slavery. It was really a step in the evolution of the system, and the limit of ten years was by no means observed. "The only legal recognition of the law was in the series of acts beginning January 4, 1703, to control the wandering of Indian and African slaves and servants, and another beginning in April, 1708, in which the slave-trade was indirectly legalized by being taxed." * "In course of time Rhode Island became the greatest slave-trader in the country, becoming a sort of clearing-house for the other colonies." †

(i) New Hampshire. This colony, profiting by the experience of its neighbor, Massachusetts, deemed it best from the beginning to discourage slavery. There were so few Negroes in the colony as to form a quantity almost negligible. Still, the system of slavery was recognized, an act being passed in 1714 to regulate the conduct of slaves, and another four years later to regulate the conduct of masters.

(j) North Carolina. In this colony, even more than in most of the others, the system of Negro slavery was long controlled by custom rather than by legal enactment. It was recognized by law in 1715, however, and police laws to govern the life of slaves were enacted.

(k) South Carolina. The history of slavery in South Carolina is peculiarly noteworthy. The natural resources of this colony offered a ready home for the system, and the laws here formulated were as explicit as any ever enacted. Slaves were first imported from Barbadoes, and their status received official confirmation in 1682. By 1720 the number had increased to 12,000, the white people numbering only 9,000.

* Alexander, 136. † DuBois, 34.

By 1698 such was the fear from the preponderance of the Negro population that a special act was passed to encourage white immigration. Legislation "for the better ordering of slaves" was made in 1690, and in 1712 the first regular slave law was enacted. Once before 1713, the year of the Assiento Contract of the Peace of Utrecht, and several times after this date, prohibitive duties were placed on Negroes to guard against their too rapid increase. By 1734, however, importation had again reached large proportions; and in 1740, in consequence of an insurrection led by a slave named Cato, a prohibitive duty several times larger than the previous one was placed upon Negroes brought into the province. The whole system of slavery in South Carolina was very profitable, Negroes being naturally adapted to life in the lowlands.

(l) Georgia. The colony of Georgia was chartered in 1732 and actually founded the next year. Oglethorpe's idea was that the colony should be a refuge for persecuted Protestants and the debtor classes of England. Slavery was forbidden on the ground that Georgia was to defend the other English colonies from the Spaniards on the south, and that it would not be able to do this if, like South Carolina, it dissipated its energies in guarding Negro slaves. For years the development of Georgia was slow, and the prosperous condition of South Carolina constantly suggested to the planters that "the one thing need-ful" for their highest welfare was slavery. Again and again were petitions addressed to the trustees, George Whitefield being among those who most urgently advocated the innovation. Moreover, Negroes from South Carolina were sometimes hired for life, and purchases were sometimes openly made in Savannah. It was not until 1749, however, that the trustees yielded to the request. In 1755 the legislature passed an act that regulated the conduct of the slaves, and in 1765 a more regular slave code was adopted. Thus did slavery finally gain a foothold in what was destined to become one of the most important of the Southern states.

CHAPTER II

7. Servitude and Slavery.—Negro slavery was not the only sort of bondage known in America in the seventeenth and eighteenth centuries. It was in fact because of a system already in existence that it became permanently fixed in the colonies. This system was known as *servitude* or *indenture*, and it explains many of the early acts with reference to the Negroes, especially those about intermarriage with white people. Servitude was "a legalized status of Indian, white, and negro servants preceding slavery in most, if not all, of the English mainland colonies." * For the origins of the system one must go back to social conditions in England in the seventeenth century. Throughout this century the lot of the workingman, especially the agricultural laborer, left much to be desired. In the earlier years mowers received for a day's work what would be now from 8 to 25 cents. The price of wheat in 1564 had been 19s. a quarter and wages had been 7d. a day. In 1610, however, wheat was 35s. a

* *New International Encyclopedia*, Article *Slavery.*

14

quarter and wages still the same. Rents were constantly increasing moreover, and many persons per-
ished from simple starvation. In the hard times
pressing upon them many Englishmen, hearing of
the great undeveloped country of Virginia, determined
to try their lot across the seas. Hundreds, however,
were too poor to pay for their transportation, and
accordingly sold themselves into servitude for a number of years to pay for the transfer. More important
from the standpoint of the system of servitude itself,
however, was the number of persons brought hither
by involuntary means. Political offenders, vagrants,
and other criminals were thus sent to the colonies, and
many persons, especially boys and girls, were kidnapped in the streets of London and "spirited" away.
It is easy to see how by such a method as this last the
system became a highly profitable one for shipmasters
and those in connivance with them. Indentured servants were purchased by the planters in the colonies
either from kidnappers or the government, the term
of servitude being generally five or seven years; and in
the laws made for the regulation of their conduct may
be found the germ of all the slave codes of the colonies.
As having the status of an apprentice the servant
could sue in court and was even allowed "freedom
dues" at the expiration of his term. He could not
vote, however, could not bear weapons, and of course

could not hold office. The first Negroes brought to the colonies were technically servants. Generally as Negro slavery advanced white servitude declined; and "servitude became slavery when to such incidents as alienation, disfranchisement, whipping, and limited marriage, were added those of perpetual service and a denial of civil, juridical, marital and property rights as well as the denial of the possession of children." * In some colonies, even after slavery was well established, the white men and women were retained as domestic servants, some even as secretaries or tutors, the Negroes being put to work in the fields. From a purely economic point of view the inferiority of the system of indenture to that of slavery was fully apparent, and as soon as Negroes began to be imported in considerable numbers, servitude was destined to pass away. The decline of the system after the last quarter of the seventeenth century was very rapid, though it did not finally pass in all its phases before the beginning of the Revolutionary War.

8. Efforts for the Restriction of Slavery.—In spite of its great economic advantages over white servitude, the system of Negro slavery did not develop without considerable opposition. Germantown's protest against slavery, made in the year 1688, was "the first formal action ever taken against the barter in human

* *New International Encyclopedia*, Article *Slavery*.

flesh within the boundaries of the United States." *
But in other places, as well as Pennsylvania, there
soon developed moral sentiment against the institution, and it was only the working of economic forces
that finally fastened it on the colonies. Even when
an individual colony was impelled by philanthropic
motives, it had to reckon with the cupidity of English
traders. Thus before 1772 Virginia passed 33 acts
looking toward a prohibition of the importation of
slaves; but in every instance the act was disallowed by
England. In the far South, especially in South Carolina, where the Negroes soon outnumbered the white
people, constant fear of insurrections led to increas-
ingly heavy duties on slaves imported. In spite of
all such spasmodic attempts for restriction, however,
the system of Negro slavery, once well started, developed apace.

9. **Increase of Negro Population.**—Largely on account of the system of indenture, Negro slavery as an
institution developed very slowly in the seventeenth
century. It was in the eighteenth century that it
began to grow by leaps and bounds. In 1625, six
years after the first Negroes were brought to the colony, there were in Virginia only 23 Negroes, 12 male,
11 female.† In 1659 there were only 300 and in 1683

---

* Faust, I, 45.
† *Virginia Magazine of History*, VII, 364.

3,000. In 1708, however, in Virginia there were 12,000 Negroes, in 1715, 23,000, in 1756, 120,156, and in 1774, 200,000. In 1715 there were in all the colonies about 58,850.* These represented about 14 per cent. of the total population. When the first census was taken in 1790, the percentage of Negroes to total population was 19.3, 757,208 being the number in the states. Of these 697,897 were slaves, Virginia being first with 293,427, and South Carolina, Maryland, and North Carolina following with a little more than 100,000 each. The percentage has never been higher than 19.3. In the nineteenth century, except in two decades, it was constantly lowered. Thus, although in 1910 there were 9,827,763 Negroes in the United States, these represented but 10.7 per cent of the total population.

10. Status of the Slave.—What now was the exact position in society of this large addition to the body politic? The whole system of Negro slavery was distinctively an evolution. As the first Negroes were taken by pirates, the rights of ownership could not legally be given to those who purchased them; hence slavery by custom preceded slavery by statute. Little by little the colonies drifted into the sterner system. The transition is marked by such an act as that of 1652 in Rhode Island, which permitted a Negro to be

---

* Blake, 378.

bound for ten years. By the time it had become generally enacted or understood in the colonies that a
child born of slave parents should serve for life, a new
question had arisen, that of the issue of a free person
and a slave. This led Virginia in 1662 to lead the way
with an act to the effect that the status of a child
should be determined by that of the mother, which
act both gave to slavery the sanction of law and made
it hereditary. In 1705 it was enacted in Virginia that
a slave might be inventoried as real estate. As property then there was nothing to prevent a slave from
being separated from his family. Thus after nearly a
hundred years since the introduction of the first
Negroes, slave codes began to take on some degree of
definiteness and uniformity. After all, however, the
colonists found that they were not dealing with
simple property, but with human beings; thus in Virginia in 1801 on the score of humanity some attempt
seems to have been made to prevent the separation of
a young child from its mother. In Maryland moreover
the problem of the relation of the Negro slave and the
indentured white servant was unusually acute. A
section of the law of 1664, designed to discourage
intermarriage between white women and Negro
slaves, enacted that a white woman so intermarrying
should serve the master of her husband as long as her
husband lived, and that the issue of such marriages

should be slaves for life. An interesting situation now developed. In order to prolong the indenture of their white female servants, many masters encouraged them to marry Negro slaves. To prevent this a new act declared that all white women so intermarrying should be free at once, but that the minister conducting the ceremony and the master or mistress promoting the marriage were to pay a fine of ten thousand pounds of tobacco. In the other Southern colonies the rule in the matter of the child of the Negro father and the indentured white mother was that the child should be bound in servitude for thirty or thirty-one years. With the passing of the system of servitude, however, passed also for the most part the intermarriage of the races. As a slave the Negro had none of the ordinary civil or personal rights of a citizen. In a criminal case he could be arrested, tried, and condemned with but one witness against him, and he could be sentenced without a jury. In the matter of religion and baptism a peculiar problem arose. Zealous for religion as the colonists were, they made little attempt to convert the Negroes in the earlier decades of the seventeenth century, there being a very general opinion that neither Christian brotherhood nor the law of England would justify the holding of Christians as slaves. In course of time, however, they lost their scruples, and it became

generally understood that conversion and baptism did not make a slave free, Virginia in 1667
enacting a law to this effect. Generally it was
only on the economic side that hope remained
for the slave. Sometimes he was allowed to
hire out his time. If he earned more than the
sum (about $100) yearly due his master, he
might begin to accumulate a little money on
his own account and ultimately purchase his freedom. Such cases, however, were exceptional. To the
great mass of Negroes in the colonies the outlook appeared hopeless enough. Their general situation before the courts may be illustrated from the history of
New York. The slave code of this colony was harsh,
and there seems to have been here a constant fear of
insurrections. One such uprising was attempted in
the city of New York in 1712. In 1741 this place was
the scene of a most unhappy panic. The city was
then a thriving town of ten thousand inhabitants.
Nine fires in rapid succession brought the city to a
state of terror and to the belief that the free Negroes
and slaves were conspiring to burn the city. Every
one of the eight lawyers in the town appeared against
the Negroes, who had no counsel and who were convicted on most insufficient evidence. The prosecu-
tions extended through the whole summer, and before
the fury subsided fourteen of the unfortunate people

were burned at the stake, eighteen were hanged, and seventy-one deported.*

11. Free Negroes in the Colonies.—Along with the general increase of the Negro population grew also the class of free persons of color. A Negro gained his freedom in one of several ways. Sometimes a scrupulous master at his death gave several of his slaves their liberty. Occasionally a slave became free by reason of some act of service to the commonwealth, as in the case of one Will, slave belonging to Robert Ruffin, of the county of Surry in Virginia, who in 1710 divulged a conspiracy.† There is moreover on record a case of an indentured Negro servant, one John Geaween, who by his unusual thrift in the matter of some hogs which he raised on the share system with his master, was able as early as 1641 to purchase his own son from another master, to the perfect satisfaction of all concerned.‡ Noteworthy also in this connection are those persons, a very large class, the descendants of Negro fathers and indentured white mothers, who ordinarily gained their freedom after thirty or thirty-one years of service. Thus in one way or another the number of free persons of color increased. When the first census was taken in 1790,

* The story is fully told by Williams, I, 144–170.
† Hening, III, 537.
‡ *Virginia Magazine of History*, X, 281.

they formed nearly 8 per cent. of the total Negro
population of the states, numbering 59,311. The
position of these people was a very anomalous one. In
the South all sorts of restrictive laws were placed upon
them, but, with the exception of those pertaining to
civil rights, these were frequently disregarded. In
Virginia free Negroes seem to have had the privilege
of voting until 1723, for an act of this year deprived
them of it. Generally in the South Negroes could
not vote, could not bear civil office, could not give
testimony in court in cases involving white men, and
could be employed only for fatigue duty in the militia.
They could not purchase white servants, could not
intermarry with white people, and had also to be
very circumspect in their personal relations with
slaves. No deprivation of privilege, however, relieved
them of the obligation to pay taxes. Such advantages
as the free Negro possessed were mainly economic.
The money gained from his labor was his own; he
might become skilled at a trade; he might buy land;
he might buy slaves; he might even buy his wife and
child if, as most frequently happened, they were
slaves; and he might have one gun with which to protect his home.* Once in a long while he might find
some private opportunity for education. In the North
his political condition was somewhat better and more

* Hening, IV, 131.

avenues for education were open to him; but along economic lines his lot was even harder than in the South.   Everywhere his position was a difficult one· He was most frequently regarded as idle and shiftless, and as a breeder of mischief; but if he showed unusual thrift he might be forced to leave his home and go elsewhere.   Liberty, the boon of every citizen, the free Negro did not possess.   For all the finer things of life—the things that make life worth living—the lot that was his was only less hard than that of the slave.

CHAPTER III

12. Character of the Age.—The period of the American Revolution in its widest limits may be made to include that of the War of 1812 as well as that of the Revolution itself. The progress of the cause of the Negro in this period is to be explained by two great forces which were being felt at the time in Europe as well as in America. One of these was the humanitarian impulse which found such abundant expression in the poems of William Cowper. The other influence was the general diffusion of liberal ideas which in England began the agitation for a free press and for parliamentary reform, which in France accounted largely for the French Revolution, and which in America led to the revolt from Great Britain. No patriot could come under the influence of either one of these forces without having his heart and his sense of justice moved to some degree in behalf of the slave.

13. Lord Mansfield's Decision.—In November, 1769, Charles Stewart, once a merchant in Norfolk and later receiver general of the customs of North America, took to England his African slave, James Somerset, who, becoming sick, was turned adrift by his master. Later Somerset recovered and Stewart seized him, intending to have him borne out of the country and sold in Jamaica. Somerset objected to this and by so doing raised the important legal question, Did a slave by being brought to England become free? The case received a great deal of attention, for everybody realized that the decision would be far-reaching in its consequences. After it was argued at three different sittings, Lord Mansfield, Chief Justice of England, in 1772 handed down from the Court of King's Bench the decision that as soon as ever any slave set his foot upon the soil of England, he became free.

14. English Sentiment.—This judgment may be taken as fairly representative of the general progress that the cause of the Negro was making in England at the time. Early in the eighteenth century sentiment against the slave-trade began to develop among the Christian people of the country. Many pamphlets telling of the evils of slavery were circulated, and as early as 1776 a motion for the abolition of the slave-trade was made in the House of Commons. John Wesley preached against the system, Adam Smith in his *Wealth of Nations* showed its ultimate expensiveness, and Edmund Burke declared that the slavery endured by the Negroes in the English settlements was worse than that ever suffered by any other people. The list of those who worked against the evil is a long one. Special mention, however, must be made of two of the greatest friends of the slave—Thomas Clarkson and William Wilberforce. Clarkson was strong in investigation and in organizing the movement against slavery, and Wilberforce was the parliamentary champion of the cause. For about twenty years, assisted by such debaters as Burke, Fox, and the younger Pitt, Wilberforce worked until on March 25th, 1807, the bill for the abolition of the slave-trade received the royal assent. Even then his work was not finished, as slavery itself was yet to be abolished in the English dominions. How this was done we shall see in a later chapter.

15. American Sentiment.—The high thought of England necessarily found reflection in America, where the logic of the position of the patriots forced them to defend the cause of liberty at all times. As early as 1774, largely through the influence of the Quakers, the first anti-slavery society was organized in Philadelphia, with Benjamin Franklin as its president. John Adams thought that "every measure of prudence ought to be assumed for the eventual total extirpation of slavery from the United States."

Thomas Jefferson denounced the system as endangering the very principle of liberty on which the state was founded, "a perpetual exercise of the most unremitting despotism on the one part, and degrading submission on the other." Patrick Henry declared of the system of slavery, "I will not—I cannot justify it! I believe a time will come when an opportunity will be offered to abolish this lamentable evil. Everything we can do is to improve it, if it happens in our day; if not, let us transmit to our descendants, together with our slaves, a pity for their unhappy lot, and an abhorrence for slavery." Washington desired nothing more than "to see some plan adopted by which slavery might be abolished by law," and ultimately liberated his own slaves. These noble sentiments made some progress, but generally the people did not respond to the high thought of the patriots. They were as yet moved by feelings of interest rather than of humanity, and in 1785, in a letter to La Fayette, Washington said that petitions for the abolition of slavery presented to the Virginia legislature could scarcely obtain a hearing.

16. The Negro in the War.—In November, 1775, Lord Dunmore, the unpopular governor of Virginia, proclaimed freedom to all slaves who would fight against the American revolutionists. He and other English leaders thought to weaken the colonies by thus depriving them of a labor supply for the throwing up of fortifications and the raising of provisions. As a result of this action, thousands of Negroes joined the British ranks. The colonies, filled with alarm, changed their attitude toward the slaves and began to permit Negroes to enlist, their masters receiving payment from the public treasury. Massachusetts, Connecticut, Rhode Island, New York, Pennsylvania, Maryland, Virginia and North Carolina thus accepted the services of slaves, and severe penalties were threatened upon those who took up arms against the American cause. It was designed to organize in the South, especially in South Carolina, an army consisting of two, three, or four battalions of Negroes. Colonel Laurens of the Continental Army had charge of the project. Able-bodied slaves were to be paid for by Congress at the rate of $1,000 each, and a slave who served well to the end of the war was to receive his freedom and $50 in addition. South Carolina and Georgia, distrustful of the plan, did not encourage or co-operate with Laurens; so he did not succeed in his work. Williams estimates that altogether about three thousand Negroes served in the American army. Generally, however, the war had little effect on the lot of the Negroes. At the close of the conflict New York, Rhode Island, and Virginia freed their slave soldiers; but for the most part the system remained as before, the English being bound by the treaty of peace not to carry away any Negroes. The race furnished several individual heroes in the war, however; and some of these will receive mention in our chapter on "The Negro as a Soldier."

17. Early Steps toward Abolition.—Various tendencies in the history of the colonies with reference to the slave-trade may be observed. From 1638 to 1664 there was a tendency to take a moral stand against the traffic, as in the laws of New England, the plan for the settlement of Georgia, and the early protest from the Germans in Pennsylvania. The period 1664–1760 was marked by the steady growth of a spirit opposed to the long continuance of the traffic, and observable in various prohibitive duties. From 1760 to 1787 there were pronounced efforts to regulate or totally prohibit the trade.* The Continental Congress made a general declaration against the importation of slaves, and the first draft of the Declaration of Independence arraigned Great Britain as the real promoter of slavery in America. The Articles of Confederation in 1781 gave the states the power to regulate this as every other form of commerce. In 1784 the Congress, assembled in Philadelphia, made a declaration of colonial rights. Fourteen articles were

---

* This statement of tendencies is from DuBois, *Suppression of the Slave-Trade*, 39.

agreed on as forming the basis of an "American Asso-ciation." In one the slave-trade was denounced and entire abstinence from it and from any trade with those concerned in it was enjoined on the members of the Association. For more definite enactments we must turn to the work of the several states. Virginia by protest in 1772, Connecticut by statute in 1774, and Delaware by her Constitution in 1776 attempted to stop the slave-trade; and Virginia in 1778 was the first political community to prohibit it with efficient penalties. Delaware's article against the slave-trade was the first such in a state Constitution; but, as we shall see later, it is to Vermont, that was still a terri-tory at this time, that the honor of taking the first step for the real abolition of slavery belongs. In 1782 the old Virginia statute forbidding emancipation ex-cept for meritorious services was repealed. The repeal was in force for ten years, in which time private emancipations were numerous. Maryland soon passed acts similar to those in Virginia prohibiting the further introduction of slaves and removing restraints on emancipation. New York and New Jersey followed the example of Virginia and Maryland in prohibiting the further introduction of slaves either from Africa or from some other states, but general emancipation was not declared in these states for many years. In 1780, in spite of considerable opposition because of the course of the Revolutionary War, the Pennsylvania Assembly passed an act forbidding the further introduction of slaves, and giving freedom to all persons thereafter born in the state. Similar provisions were enacted in Connecticut and Rhode Island in 1784. In Massachusetts as early as 1701 the town of Boston had instructed its representatives in the general assembly to propose "putting an end to Negroes being slaves." This province was much agitated about slavery from 1766 to 1773, and frequent attempts were made to restrict further importations of Negro slaves. In this period a Negro took his case before the Supreme Court to decide the question, Under the laws of Massachusetts could a Negro be a slave? His argument was that the royal charter declared that all persons residing in the province were to be as free as the king's subjects in Great Britain, that by Magna Charta no subject could be deprived of liberty except by the judgment of his peers, and that any laws that may have been passed in the province attempting to mitigate or regulate the evil of slavery did not authorize it. This Negro was financially supported by others, and he was awarded a favorable decision. The judgment, however, failed to have any general effect, and at the beginning of the Revolution the Congress of Massachusetts seemed to recognize the system of slavery by the decision that no slave could be enlisted in the army. In 1777, however, some slaves brought from Jamaica were ordered to be set at liberty, and it was finally decided in 1783 that the declaration in the Massachusetts Bill of Rights to the effect that "all men are born free and equal" prohibited slavery. In this year New Hampshire incorporated in her constitution an article definitely prohibiting slavery. Far different was the course of events in the Southern States. North Carolina in 1777 enacted that instead of the consent of the governor and council that of the county court was necessary for the freedom of a slave; and neither South Carolina nor Georgia took any steps to encourage emancipation. It will be seen, however, from this rapid review that some progress had been made. By the time the convention for the framing of the Constitution of the United States met in Philadelphia in 1787, at least two of the original thirteen states (Massachusetts and New Hampshire) had positively prohibited slavery, and in three others (Pennsylvania, Connecticut, and Rhode Island) gradual abolition was in progress.

18. The Northwest Territory.—The Northwest Territory was the region west of Pennsylvania, east of the Mississippi River, north of the Ohio River, and south of Canada, finally organized in 1787 as a territory of the United States. At the outbreak of the

Revolutionary War this region was claimed by Virginia, New York, Connecticut, and Massachusetts. This territory afforded to these states a source of revenue not possessed by the others for the payment of debts incurred in the war. Maryland and other seaboard states insisted that in order to equalize matters these claimants should cede their rights to the general government. The formal cessions were made and accepted in the years 1782–6. In April, 1784, after Virginia had made her cession, the most important, Congress adopted a temporary form of government drawn up by Thomas Jefferson for the territory south as well as north of the Ohio River. Jefferson's most significant provision, however, was rejected. This declared that "after the year 1800 there shall be neither slavery nor involuntary servitude in any of the said states other than in the punishment of crimes whereof the party shall have been duly convicted." In 1787 the last Continental Congress, however, passed "An Ordinance for the Government of the Territory of the United States, Northwest of the Ohio," the Southern states not having ceded the area south of the river. It was declared that "There shall be neither slavery nor involuntary servitude in the said territory, otherwise than in punishment of crimes, whereof the parties shall be duly convicted." To this was added the stipulation (soon afterwards embodied in the federal Constitution) for the delivery of fugitives from labor or service. In this shape the ordinance was adopted, even South Carolina and Georgia concurring. Thus was paved the way for the first fugitive slave law.

19. The Constitution and Slavery.—Slavery was the cause of two of the three great compromises that characterized the making of the Constitution of the United States (the third, which was the first made, being the concession to the smaller states of equal representation in the Senate). These are the first of a long list of compromises in the history of the subject. South Carolina, with able representatives, largely dominated the thought of the convention, threatening not to accept the Constitution if there was not some compliance with her demands. An important question was that of representation, the Southern states advocating representation according to numbers, slave and free, while the Northern states were in favor of the representation of free persons only. It was finally agreed to reckon three-fifths of the slaves in estimating taxes and to make taxation the basis of representation. With reference to the slave-trade a bargain was made between the commercial interests of the North and the slaveholding interests of the South, the granting to Congress of unrestricted power to enact navigation laws being conceded in exchange for twenty years' continuance of the African slave-trade. The main agreements on the subject of slavery were thus finally expressed in the Constitution: "Representatives and direct taxes shall be apportioned among the several states which may be included within this Union, according to their respective numbers, which shall be determined by adding to the whole number of free persons, including those bound to servitude for a term of years, and excluding Indians not taxed, three-fifths of all other persons" (Art. I, Sec. 2); "The migration or importation of such persons as any of the states now existing shall think proper to admit, shall not be prohibited by the congress prior to the year 1808; but a tax or duty may be imposed, not exceeding ten dollars on each person" (Art. I, Sec. 9); "No person held to service or labor in one state, under the laws thereof, escaping into another, shall, in consequence of any law or regulation therein, be discharged from such service or labor, but shall be delivered up on claim of the party to whom such service or labor may be due" (Art. IV, Sec. 2). It will be observed that the word *slaves* occurs in no one of these articles. The framers of the Constitution did not wish to have their document recognize property in human beings.

20. Inventions.—Of incalculable significance in the history of the Negro in America was the series of inventions of the years 1767–93. In 1768 Richard Arkwright, after a year of experimenting, set up in Preston in England his first spinning-frame, which consisted mainly of two pairs of revolving rollers. About 1764 James Hargreaves of England invented the spinning-jenny. In 1779 the principles of these two inventions were utilized by Samuel Crompton in his spinning-mule, which had as its distinctive feature a spindle-carriage which, receding so as to ease the strain of winding on the spindles, produced yarn suitable for the manufacture of fine muslins. In this same period the revolutionary discovery of the power of steam by James Watt of Glasgow was applied to cotton manufacture, and improvements were made in printing and bleaching. There yet remained one final invention of importance for the cultivation and manufacture of cotton on a large scale. Eli Whitney, a graduate of Yale, went to Georgia and was employed by the widow of General Greene on her plantation. Seeing the need of some machine for the more rapid separating of cotton-seed from the fiber, he labored until in 1793 he succeeded in making his cotton gin of practical value. The tradition is persistent, however, that the real credit for the invention belongs to a Negro on the plantation. The cotton-gin created great excitement throughout the South and began to be utilized everywhere. The cultivation and export-

ing of the staple grew by leaps and bounds. Thus at
the very time that the Northern states were abolishing
slavery, an industry that had slumbered became supreme, and the fate of hundreds of thousands of Negro
slaves was sealed.

21. Influence of Toussaint L'Ouverture.—About
this time there came into the notice of the world a
remarkable man whose influence on the history of
slavery in the United States has yet to be fully estimated. The most important colonial possession of
France was Santo Domingo, which then included
also the present Hayti. Hither slaves had been
brought in such numbers that in 1791 there were on
the island sixteen Negroes to one white man. The
French slave code was not harsh; but its provisions
were generally disregarded by the planters on the
island. The result of this and of a vacilating attitude
on the part of the Assembly in Paris was that in 1794
Toussaint L'Ouverture, the leader of Negro insur-
gents, became supreme on the island as commander-
in-chief. British soldiers invited by the planters were
forced to leave in 1798. Toussaint as president
brought the island to a high degree of prosperity; but
in 1802 he was treacherously seized by the emissaries
of Napoleon Bonaparte, taken to France, and confined
in a dungeon. This was the man who caused France
to lose her most important colonial possession, and

the Negro race to obtain its first independent settlement outside of the continent of Africa. In America
the influence of this chieftain strengthened the anti-
slavery movement, became one of the reasons for the
cheap selling of Louisiana, and rendered more certain
the prohibition of the slave-trade by the United
States in 1807.* A wave of fear swept over the South,
and the voice of morality began to speak more loudly
than that of trade to the New England conscience.
The effect on legislation was immediate, South Carolina, North Carolina, and Georgia passing more repressive measures, directed especially against importations of West Indian Negroes.

22. From **1789 to 1817. New States and Territories.**—In Washington's administration considerable
discussion grew out of different memorials presented
to Congress for the suppression of the slave-trade.
These generally emanated from the Quakers in Pennsylvania, who were untiring in their efforts for the
slave. A fugitive slave law was passed in 1793. It
practically placed the burden of proof on the fugitive;
accordingly many free Negroes were remanded into
slavery. As many of the Northern states passed acts
forbidding their magistrates to take any part in putting this law into execution, it became substantially a
dead letter; nevertheless its moral force was to

* See DuBois, 70.

strengthen the South. A measure of 1794 in Congress was the first national act against the slave-trade. It was designed to prevent the carrying on of the traffic from the United States to any foreign place or country, or the fitting out of slavers in the United States for any such place or country. Vermont was admitted to the Union in 1791. Her constitution, originally adopted in 1777, declared very positively against slavery; so that to this state really belongs the honor of being the first to prohibit and abolish slavery. Kentucky was formally admitted in 1792, the article on slavery in her constitution encouraging the system and discouraging emancipation. Tennessee entered as a slave state in 1796. In 1797 the question of slavery in the Mississippi Territory was raised, and the only restraint placed here was that Negroes should not be brought in from outside of the United States. In 1798 the Constitution of Georgia was revised. On the matter of slavery it followed the Kentucky article making emancipation difficult. In 1799, after many efforts and much debating, New York at last declared for gradual abolition. As frequent mention has been made of this matter of gradual abolition, and as New York's solution of the problem was fairly typical, it might be well to review the chief provisions in her act. Those who were slaves were to continue such for life. Their children born after the following

July 4th were to be free, but were to remain as apprentices with the owner of the mother, the men until they were twenty-eight years old, the women until they were twenty-five. The exportation of slaves was forbidden, and the slave on whom such an attempt was made was to be set free at once. Persons coming into the state might bring with them slaves whom they had owned for a year previously; but slaves so brought in could not be sold. New Jersey declared for gradual abolition in 1804. It was not until about 1830, however, that slavery finally ceased in New York, and still later than this in New Jersey. Attempts were made about 1800 for gradual abolition in Kentucky and Maryland; but these failed, as did also an attempt for more speedy emancipation in Pennsylvania. In 1802 Georgia ceded to the United States the territory now comprising Alabama and Mississippi, exacting for this, however, an article favorable to slavery. When in 1803 Ohio was carved out of the Northwest Territory as a free state, an attempt was made to claim the rest of the territory for slavery; but this did not succeed. In the congressional session of 1804–5 the matter of slavery in the newly acquired territory of Louisiana was brought up, and slaves were allowed to be imported from other states if they had come to the United States not later than 1798, the intention of this last clause being to guard against a recent act of South Carolina reviving the slave-trade. In this latter state importation, prohibited in 1787, was again legalized in 1803; and in the four years immediately following 39,075 Negroes were brought to Charleston.* As the constitutional twenty-year period of the prohibition of measures against the slave-trade was expiring, there were animated debates in Congress on the subject. At length it was enacted that the importation of slaves should be prohibited after December 31, 1807. As we shall see, although this act went into effect, the slave-trade was by no means suppressed. Smuggling was continued, sometimes on a large scale. Louisiana was admitted as a slave state in 1812, and Indiana came into the Union in 1816. The subject of slavery was generally quiescent in the period of the War of 1812. This war was opposed by the South; just why may be seen from the fact that Admiral Cochrane of the British navy issued an address designed especially to attract slaves to his standard. The war, moreover, was damaging to the exportation of cotton. Mississippi was admitted to the Union December 10, 1817, slavery being recognized in a clause not granting to slaves the privilege of trial by jury. Illinois entered in 1818, and Alabama in 1819. It will be observed that up to this time the balance had been fairly well

* The figure is from DuBois, 90.

preserved between the slave and the free states. Of the former there were in the original thirteen seven, and of the latter six. Vermont was an addition to the free states; but the admission of Kentucky and Tennessee strengthened the South. Then from 1803 to 1819 Ohio and Louisiana, Indiana and Mississippi, and Illinois and Alabama marked an alternation of free and slave states. The Southern states soon realized that they could not long maintain this balance because of the lack of territory and also by reason of the fact that the business of the North tended more than that of the South to the rapid growth of population. In the meantime came the application of Missouri for entrance; but with this event the history of slavery started on a new era, one destined not to be closed until the Negro was free.

23. The Decline of Great Convictions.—We have seen that at the beginning of this period liberal ideas were dominant in both England and America. One of the sad features of the close of the era is the fading of the ideals that had inspired the patriots of the Revolution. Generally the energies of the young nation were being directed to the material development of the country, and more commercial interests entered into the second war with Great Britain than into the first. In the North there was a lull in the agitation, the meetings of anti-slavery organizations becoming intermittent. In the South the men of patriotism and responsibility found themselves in the grasp of a mighty evil which it was almost as difficult to shake off as to endure. Generally the demands of interest were taking precedence over those of humanity; and Virginia, North Carolina, and South Carolina made more stringent laws against emancipation. Increasing sensitiveness on the subject of slavery was felt, and Thomas Jefferson, apostle of democracy, dared not risk his popularity by utterances similar to those of his earlier life. Considerable advance had been made, however. Four states (Massachusetts, New Hampshire, Vermont, and Ohio) had definitely prohibited slavery, and generally throughout the North abolition was in progress.

CHAPTER IV

24. General View of the System.—It is now time to look somewhat more intimately at the actual working of the system which has really formed the subject of the last two chapters. "In colonies like those in the West Indies and in South Carolina and Georgia, the rapid importation into America of a multitude of savages gave rise to a system of slavery far different from that which the late Civil War abolished. The strikingly harsh and even inhuman slave codes in those colonies show this. Crucifixion, burning, and starvation were legal modes of punishment. The rough and brutal character of the time and place was largely responsible for this; but a more decisive reason lay in the fierce and turbulent character of the imported Negroes. . . . On the other hand, in New England and New York the Negroes were merely house servants or farm hands, and were treated neither better nor worse than servants in general in those days. Between these two extremes, the system of slavery varied from a mild serfdom in Pennsylvania and New Jersey to an aristocratic caste system in Maryland and Virginia." *

25. Procuring Slaves.—As to the actual procuring of the slaves, the process was by no means as easy as is sometimes supposed. The captain of a vessel had to resort to various expedients in order to get his cargo. His commonest method was to bring with him a variety of gay cloth, cheap ornaments, and whiskey, which he would give in exchange for slaves brought to him. His task was most simple when a chieftain of one tribe brought to him several hundred prisoners of war. Most often, however, the work was more toilsome, and kidnapping a favorite method, though, as is commonly thought, individuals were frequently enticed on vessels. The work was always dangerous, for the natives along the slave coast were suspicious. After they had seen some of their fellows taken away, they learned not to go unarmed while a slave-vessel was on the coast, and very often there were hand-to-hand encounters. "At first the slave vessels only visited the Guinea coast, and bargained with the negroes of the villages there for what quantity of wax, or gold, or negroes they had to give. But this was a clumsy way of conducting business. The ships had to sail along a large tract of coast, picking up a few negroes at one place, and a little ivory or gold at an-

* DuBois, 5, 6.

other; sometimes even the natives of a village might have no elephants' teeth and no negroes to give; and even under the most favorable circumstances it took a considerable time to procure a decent cargo. No coast is so pestilential as that of Africa, and hence the service was very repulsive and very dangerous. As an improvement on this method of trading, the plan was adopted very early of planting small settlements of Europeans at intervals along the slave-coast, whose business it should be to negotiate with the negroes, stimulate them to activity in the slave-hunting expeditions, purchase the slaves brought in, and warehouse them until the arrival of the ships. These settlements were called slave factories. Factories of this kind were planted all along the western coast from Cape Verde to the equator, by English, French, Dutch, and Portuguese traders." *

26. The Middle Passage.—Once on board the slaves were put in chains two by two. When the ship was ready to start, the hold of the vessel, whose ceiling might be four feet from the floor, would be crowded with moody and unhappy wretches who most commonly were made to crouch so that their knees touched their chins. There was one entrance to the hold, and there were small gratings on the sides. The clothing of a slave, if there was any at all, consisted of a rag

* Blake, 99.

about the loins. The food consisted of rice, yams, beans, or soup, and sometimes bread and meat; but the cooking was not good, nor was any care taken to see that all the slaves were fed. The supply of water was always limited, a pint a day being a generous allowance. For exercise the slaves were made to dance by the lash, and in order that they might be less gloomy they were also frequently forced to sing. The rule was to bring them on deck for an airing twice a day, about eight o'clock in the morning and four in the afternoon.

27. Effects of Treatment on Slaves.—On board the vessel not all the slaves were quiet by any means. Many instances of stubborn resistance are on record. Sustenance was frequently refused in order that death might be hastened. Sleeping conditions were horrible. Throughout the night the hold resounded with the moans of those who awoke from dreams of home to find themselves in bonds. The women frequently became hysterical, and both men and women sometimes became insane. Fearful and contagious diseases sometimes broke out. Small-pox was one of these. Much more common was ophthalmia, a frightful inflammation of the eyes. A blind (hence worthless) slave was generally thrown to the sharks. Many of the victims would embrace any opportunity that might be presented to leap overboard in the hope (that universally

prevailed among them) of being taken back to Africa.
The sanitary conditions of the vessel can better be
imagined than described. The slaves, bound for
hours, together, wallowed in inconceivable filth. The
putrid atmosphere, sudden transitions from heat to
cold, and melancholy increased the mortality among
a people naturally light-hearted; and frequently when
morning came a dead and a living slave were found
shackled together. A captain always counted on
losing on the voyage one-fourth of his cargo of slaves.

28. Effects on Seamen.—The physical effects of the
system on the common seamen were only less bad
than those on the slaves. These men were often
naturally brutal, but not always. Sometimes they accepted work on a slaver as a last resort before going
to jail. One who remembers the condition of English
prisons in the earlier part of the eighteenth century
will not wonder that the men accepted any possible
alternative. The life of the seamen brought them
into close contact with the slaves, whose contagious
diseases they readily contracted. They received harsh
treatment from the captain of the vessel, who was
invariably a man of blunted sympathies. That the
slave-trade was not relished by the men who had to
do the dirty work may be seen from the difficulty of
getting men for the service and from the large number
of desertions.

29. Price of Slaves.—When a cargo of slaves was once in port, an auction would very soon be announced. In the earlier years the price of a slave was far less than what it became just before the Civil War; but consideration must be given to the greater purchasing power of money than in the later period. About the year 1700 able-bodied adult Negroes were valued at from $125 to $200, and children at $50 or $60. There was little difference in the value of men and women, for while a man might do more work, a woman might beget children for her master. A man worth $200 would in one or two seasons by his labor bring back to his owner the amount of money expended for him. After the invention of the cotton-gin the price of slaves rose so that a man who in 1792 brought $300 sold in 1800 for $450. The price continued to rise until in the middle of the nineteenth century that for an able-bodied man or a beautiful woman was very frequently $1,200, and, under exceptional circumstances, even $1,800. A slave was regarded as personal property, and to steal one was a capital offense.

30. Work of Slaves.—Slaves were of most value when large numbers of them worked together. In the South the tendency was to develop large plantations. One thousand was the number of slaves on the ordinary large plantation, though once in a while the figure became as high as four or even five thousand. In Virginia and Kentucky tobacco was raised. In South Carolina the cultivation of rice began about 1693. By 1740 the yield was worth $1,000,000 a year. For a long time indigo was next to this staple in importance. Some silk, flax, hemp, oranges, corn, and sugar were also raised; but, as we have seen, after the invention of the cotton-gin cotton became supreme. The law with reference to slaves on plantations imposed a penalty of £5 if they were made to work on Sunday or more than fifteen hours a day in summer or fourteen in winter. This was for the colonial period; the same general limits obtained in later years. Such skilled labor as the South possessed before the Civil War was mainly in the hands of slaves, who might be blacksmiths, harness-makers, carpenters, or similar artisans. Generally, however, work in the trades was such as was incident to plantation life. Almost nothing in the way of manufactures was done in the South; and it was because goods were imported from England and the North that Charleston was for so long a time a city of commanding importance.

31. Plantation Life.—The plantation hand lived in the "quarters," a collection of rude, dilapidated cabins. His own room, which he shared with others, contained an apology for a bed, a chair or two, a frying-pan, a kettle, and a pot-rack. The walls were adorned with one or two gaudy pictures. No wardrobe was necessary as there was nothing to put in one. An average allowance of food for a plantation hand was a peck and a half of meal and three pounds of bacon a week. In Louisiana the law required a planter to give a slave 200 pounds of pork a year. Generally the slave had also some potatoes and green vegetables. The following picture of life on a Virginia plantation may be taken as fairly representative of the system in its milder aspects: "After breakfast has been eaten in the cabins, at sunrise or a little before in winter, and perhaps a little later in summer, they [the slaves] go to the field. At noon dinner is brought to them, and, unless the work presses, they are allowed two hours' rest. Very punctually at sunset they stop work and are at liberty, except that a squad is detached once a week for shelling corn, to go to the mill for the next week's drawing of meal. Thus they work in the field about eleven hours a day on an average. Returning to the cabins, wood 'ought to have been' carted for them; but if it has not been, they then go to the woods and 'tote' it home for themselves. They then make a fire . . . and cook their own supper, which will be a bit of bacon fried, often with eggs, cornbread baked in the spider after the bacon, to absorb the fat, and perhaps some sweet potatoes roasted in the ashes.

Immediately after supper they go to sleep, often lying on the floor or a bench in preference to a bed. About two o'clock they very generally rouse up and cook and eat, or eat cold, what they call their 'mornin' bit'; and sleep again till breakfast." *

32. Slave Breeding.—For a long time it cost as much to raise a slave as he would ultimately be worth, and it was commonly thought to be cheaper to buy slaves than to rear them. The legal abolition of the slave-trade, however, coinciding with the heavy demands imposed by the Louisiana Purchase and the development of the lower South, greatly changed matters. The slave increased in value, and Virginia and Maryland became famous breeding places for the plantations of the far South, a woman who was an extraordinary breeder being advertised as such. In 1832 the apologist for slavery wrote: "Virginia is, in fact, a *negro* raising state for other states; she produces enough for her own supply, and six thousand for sale." † "For the ten years preceding 1860 the average annual importation of slaves into the seven Southern states from the slave-breeding states was little less than twenty-five thousand." ‡ On remote plantations the operation of the system was most

---

* Olmstead, *Journey in the Seaboard Slave States*, 109.

† Dew, in the *Pro-Slavery Argument*, 359.

‡ Olmstead, *The Cotton Kingdom*, I, 58.

gross; and a woman separated from her husband was forced to accept a new mate.

33. Religion.—Of the slaves who came to America a very few of the first were Mohammedans and could even read the Koran. Most of them, however, were densely ignorant and very superstitious. They remained illiterate in this country as, except in some places in the North, it was a crime to teach a slave to read. On the matter of religion for the Negro, however, there seems in the later years to have been sufficient concern. Indeed it was in the thought that in America the slave was brought into the light of Christianity that benevolent people solaced themselves for the whole system of slavery. Generally in cities slaves were expected to go to church. They occupied a corner or a gallery. On plantations it was very common for the slaves to have a meeting on Sunday; and it was at this that the "exhorter" of the plantation fulfilled his wonted function. The law required that at least one white person should be present at any such meetings of slaves. In actual practice an overseer simply passed by and looked in for a moment to see what was being done. Much of the worship of the slaves was simply the cultivation of emotional frenzy; but here and there light shone in the darkness and the true gospel was preached. The

Negro Church was born nearly a hundred years before the Civil War.

34. Laws Concerning Slaves.—When it is remembered that each state had its own slave code, it will be seen that it is a difficult matter to make general statements about the legal side of slavery. The slave was by law due support in age or sickness, a right to limited religious instruction, and the privileges of marrying, having some free time, and testifying in cases concerning other slaves. If he did not get what was due him he had no redress, for he had no legal voice. His marriage was not considered binding and he was not supposed to have any morals, although many individuals were models of integrity and faithfulness. In New England slaves were regarded as possessing the same legal rights as apprentices, and if masters abused their authority they were liable to indictment. The code of South Carolina may be taken as representative of the harsher ones. According to this a slave could not leave a plantation without a ticket of leave from his master; if he had no passport he might be given twenty lashes, or be "moderately punished" by a man that stopped him, or be regarded as a fugitive; he could have no firearms or other weapons in his possession; nor (for fear of poisonings) was he allowed to make any medicines without the knowledge of his master or mistress. On plantations no master was to allow a slave to plant for himself any

corn, peas, or rice, or keep any private stock; and
generally slaves were to wear clothes of the coarsest
material only. Such provisions as these last, however, were commonly disregarded.

35. Punishment.—By the South Carolina act of
1740 a fine of £700 was imposed for the deliberate
murder of a slave by his master or another white
man, £350 for killing him under correction or in the
heat of passion, and £100 for mutilation or cruel punishment. In Mississippi it was decided in 1820 that
the wanton killing of a slave by his master was murder.
In Georgia, however, it was declared thirty years
later that a master had absolute power over a slave.
In actual practice, as plantations were remote and as
a slave had no legal voice, no penalty was anywhere
attached to the murder of a slave by his master,
though of course the owner could recover damages if
his slave was killed by anybody else. Severe cruelties
for petty offenses were imposed by the South Carolina
code of 1712; but these were soon modified, and in
actual practice the punishment for stealing was generally whipping. In Charleston and elsewhere just
before the Civil War the common punishment of a
slave for a minor offense was ten lashes on the bare
back. This was administered by a man who made it
his business to whip slaves and who rendered his
monthly account to his patrons at the rate of ten

lashes for fifteen cents. It is needless to say that the slaves regarded this man as their inveterate enemy. If resistance was offered, the punishment was doubled or trebled. After these inflictions the flesh was commonly left raw. "The ordinary death penalty for the black man was hanging. Burning at the stake was not unknown, but there is one instance of such an execution in Massachusetts, and there are several in New York, so that it can not be cited as illustrating any peculiarity of the South Carolina type of slavery." *

36. Peculiar Social Aspects.—In the study of slavery, as in the study of any other institution, it is to be remembered that peculiar attendant circumstances were ever present to modify large deductions that might be made. One thing that has been touched upon more than once in the course of these pages was the differing character of the system of slavery in different states, even in different Southern states. On the great plantations along the coast or in the cotton belt slavery appeared in all its grossness and hideousness. In Virginia, however, there was originally a more patriarchal form of the system; and the mistress of the estate not infrequently became the nurse of all the slaves on the plantation. Another attendant circumstance to be reckoned with is the fact that in numberless instances the masters of plantations or

* Fiske, II, 330.

estates themselves became the fathers of slaves. Most frequently their children fared just as any other slaves; but not always. Such incidents as these, however, but emphasize the evil effects of slavery on both the dominant and the subject race.

37. Argument for Slavery.—Deserving at least of passing notice in this review are the arguments advanced by the South in support of slavery. The foremost apologist for the system, a professor at William and Mary College, argued that slavery had made for the civilization of the world in that it had mitigated the evils of war, had made labor profitable, had changed the nature of savages, and elevated woman. The slave-trade was of course horrible and unjust; but the great advantages of the system more than outweighed a few attendant evils. Emancipation and deportation were impossible. Even if practicable, they would be inexpedient measures, for they meant the loss to Virginia of one-third of her property. As for morality, it was not to be expected that the Negro should have the sensibilities of the white man. Moreover, the system had the positive advantage of cultivating a republican spirit among the white people. In short, said Dew, the slaves, in both the economic and the moral point of view, were "entirely unfit for a state of freedom among the whites." These arguments the church, with its usual conservatism, supported. It was pointed out that the old Mosaic law recognized slavery, that in the New Testament servants were told to be obedient to their masters, and that, best of all, the Apostle Paul was on the side of the fugitive slave law, having advised the servant Onesimus to go back to his master Philemon. Moreover, Jesus Christ had on no occasion spoken against slavery. Just before the war a distinguished minister, Palmer of New Orleans, preached a noteworthy sermon which was printed and sent broadcast over the country. He maintained in substance that such an overturning of the established order of things as the opponents of slavery intended was not only a violation of the Constitution of the United States, but the very endeavor to bring about a new reign of anarchy in society. After the lapse of years the pro-slavery argument is pitiful in its numerous fallacies, and it but serves as an example of the extremes to which economic interest will sometimes force men of the highest intelligence and honor.

38. Economy of Slavery.—We have seen that on its own confession the colony of Georgia did not begin to grow until it used slave labor. In course of time the very life of the South came to depend on the cotton industry. The final economic effects of the system of slavery on this section, however, were disastrous. "It needed no extensive marshalling of statistics to prove that the welfare of the North was greater than that of the South. Two simple facts, everywhere admitted, were of so far-reaching moment that they amounted to irrefragable demonstration. The emigration from the slave states was much larger than the movement in the other direction; and the South repelled the industrious emigrants who came from Europe, while the North attracted them." *

The rich men of the South, moreover, invested their capital in land and slaves, so that mercantile interests passed into the hands of Northerners and Englishmen; and in course of time the South became wholly dependent on places outside of herself for manufactured goods. This fact accounts for South Carolina's attitude toward the tariff of 1828 and her emphasis on the principle of nullification. At a time when on account of increased production cotton was falling in value from forty cents a pound to seven or eight cents, this same cotton was coming back from England as cloth or clothing under a very high tariff. It was the rich planter rather than the white man of slender means who profited by slavery, wealth being more and more concentrated in a few hands. Among those white people who did not own slaves, moreover, there grew up a contempt for industrial effort, all manual labor being associated in their minds with slavery.

* Rhodes, I, 355.

In 1860 41 per cent. of the white men who had been
born in South Carolina were living in other states.*
Some of the men of Scotch-Irish stock in the "up-
country" emigrated before the middle of the century
on account of antipathy to slavery; still more yielded
to the call of the rich lands of the West: but the great
majority of those who moved were driven away by
the competition of slave labor. More and more the
South realized that she was not keeping pace with
the country's development. Said the Richmond *En-
quirer*, one of the strongest pro-slavery organs, under
date December 25, 1852: "Virginia, anterior to the
Revolution, and up to the adoption of the Federal
Constitution, contained more wealth and a larger
population than any other state of this Confeder-
acy. . . . Virginia, from being first in point of wealth
and political power, has come down to the fifth place
in the former, and the fourth in the latter. New York,
Pennsylvania, Massachusetts, and Ohio stand above
her in wealth, and all but Massachusetts in population and political power." The apologist for slavery
might have shown more than one reason for this decline; but students of political economy agreed upon
one main cause—Slavery. It remained for a son of
the South, a representative of white men of limited
means, to expose the system. *The Impending Crisis*,

* Professor D. D. Wallace, in the Columbia *State*, August 15, 1909.

produced four years before the Civil War, was surpassed in sensational interest by no other book of
the period except *Uncle Tom's Cabin.* Hinton Rowan
Helper, the author, was from North Carolina. He
did not place himself upon the broadest principles
of humanity and statesmanship; he had little interest
in the Negro slave as such, and the great planters of
the South were to him the "whelps" and "curs" of
slavery. He spoke simply as the voice of the nonslaveholding whites of the South. He set forth such
unpleasant truths as that the personal and real property, including slaves, of Virginia, North Carolina,
Tennessee, Missouri, Arkansas, Florida, and Texas,
taken all together, was less than the real and personal
estate in the single state of New York; that the hay
crop alone of the North was worth more than all the
cotton, rice, tobacco, hay, hemp, and cane-sugar of
the South; that representation in Southern legislatures was unfair; that in the national congress a
Southern planter was twice as powerful as a Northern
man; that slavery was to blame for the migration from
the South to the West; and that in short the system of
slavery was harmful in its influence in every way. All
of this was decidedly unpleasant to the ears of the
property owners of the South; Helper's book was
proscribed, and the author himself found it more advisable to live in New York than in North Carolina.

The Impending Crisis was eagerly read, however, and it succeeded as a book because it attempted to attack with some degree of honesty a great economic problem.

CHAPTER V

39. Character of the Period.—The period 1820–60 was characterized by a career of constant aggression on the part of the slave power. This aggression was marked by five great steps: (1) the Missouri Compromise (1820), the annexation of Texas (1845), the Fugitive Slave Law (1850), the Kansas-Nebraska Bill (1854), and the Dred Scott Decision (1857). In addition to these measures in which it succeeded, the South also attempted to acquire Cuba and did actually revive the slave-trade. The mere enumeration of these measures but emphasizes the fact that slavery is the greatest subject not only in the history of the Negro race in America, but even in that of the American nation itself.

40. Missouri Compromise.—When in 1818 Missouri applied for entrance into the Union as a slave state, a great amount of debating resulted, lasting two years. In the meantime Alabama (in 1819) and Maine (in 1819) also applied for admission. Alabama was admitted without much discussion, as she made equal the number of slave and free states. Maine, however, brought forth more talk. The Southern men would have been perfectly willing to receive this as a free state if Missouri had been admitted as a slave state; but the North felt that this would have conceded altogether too much, as Missouri from the first gave promise of being unusually important. At length, largely through the influence of Henry Clay, there was adopted a compromise whose main provisions were as follows: (1) Maine was to be admitted as a free state; (2) in Missouri there was to be no prohibition of slavery; but (3) slavery was to be prohibited in other states that might be formed out of the Louisiana Purchase north of the line of 36° 30'. While the South really accomplished more than the North by the Missouri Compromise, the measure served to allay the strife for some years. It is debatable now, however, if it was a piece of wise statesmanship, and if it might not have been better to fight the battle out then once for all rather than postpone the contest for forty years. Public opinion, however, was not yet ripe on the subject of slavery.

41. Mason and Dixon's line.—This phrase was first used during the debates on the Missouri Compromise to indicate the dividing line between the slave and the free states. The Mason and Dixon's Line was really only the boundary between Pennsylvania and Maryland along the parallel of 39° 43′ 26.3″, the line of which was run in 1763-7 by two English surveyors, Charles Mason and Jeremiah Dixon, to settle a dispute between the Penn and Baltimore families. The real dividing line between the slave and the free states followed not only the southern Pennsylvania boundary, but also the Ohio River to the Mississippi, and then, with the exception of the state of Missouri, the parallel of 36° 30′ established by the Compromise. Even to-day, however, the phrase *Mason and Dixon's Line* is sometimes used to designate the line between the North and the South, and it is unfortunate that it should ever have been coined thus to divide the country geographically.

42. The Abolitionists. **Lundy, Garrison.**—The Abolitionists were those opponents of slavery who, on the ground that the system was wrong, advocated its instant extinction by any means whatsoever and without compensation to slave owners. Their movement, begun in a spirit of humanitarianism, continued until slavery no longer existed in the country. As early as the second decade of the century Benjamin Lundy, a Quaker, advocated abolitionist principles. This man was one of the most unselfish friends the slave ever had. He worked at his trade as a saddler in Wheeling, Va. (now W. Va.), and later published at various places a paper called *The Genius of Universal*

Emancipation. "Infirm, deaf, unimpressive in speech and bearing, trudging on long journeys, and accepting a decent poverty, he gave all the resources of a strong and sweet nature to the service of the friendless and unhappy." * The abolitionist movement really became aggressive, however, with the establishment in Boston January 1, 1831, by William Lloyd Garrison, of a newspaper called *The Liberator.* Garrison, one of Lundy's converts, became the leader of the agitation. In his salutatory editorial he said: "I will be as harsh as truth and as uncompromising as justice. On this subject I do not wish to think or speak or write with moderation. . . . I am in earnest—I will not equivocate—I will not excuse—I will not retreat a single inch—and I will be heard!" Quoting Isaiah xxviii, 18, he termed the Constitution "a covenant with death and an agreement with hell;" and his arraignment of the national document made enemies for him in the North as well as in the South. The Abolitionists weakened their position by their absolute refusal to countenance any laws that recognized slavery, thus repelling many conservative men; but they gained force when Congress denied them the right of petition and when President Jackson refused them the use of the United States mails. In the South they were detested and Nat Turner's insurrec-

* Merriam, 38.

tion was ascribed to their influence. In January, 1832, they established the New England Anti-Slavery Society, and in December, 1833, the American Anti-Slavery Society, which was not dissolved until 1870. The more conservative men, those who believed in using the governmental machinery in the work of abolition, organized in 1840 the Liberty party, which in 1848 became an element of the Free-Soil party, which in turn became fused in the Republican party in 1854-6.

43. Other Leaders.—Prominent among the Abolitionists were Elijah P. Lovejoy, Wendell Phillips, Theodore Parker, John Greenleaf Whittier, and Lydia Maria Child. Lovejoy, a martyr if ever there was one, in 1837 lost his life in Alton, Ill., in an attack by a mob on a building in which he published an anti-slavery paper. Wendell Phillips of Boston was one of the most polished and forceful of American orators. Working often against mobs, he delivered many speeches in behalf of the Negro. One of his most finished orations is that on Toussaint L'Ouverture. He closed his law office because he was not willing to swear that he would support the Constitution; he relinquished the franchise because he did not wish to have any personal responsibility for a government that countenanced slavery; and he lost sympathy with the Christian church because of its compromising attitude toward the system. Theodore Parker, also of Massachusetts, was a Unitarian minister who inspired many noble men and women by the courage with which he applied the principles of his religion to current political issues. Whittier was the poet of the anti-slavery cause. Such a poem as *The Slave Ships* showed forth the horrors of the slave-trade, and one like *The Farewell* showed the iniquity of separating children from their parents. Lydia Maria Child was a noble woman whose *Appeal for that Class of Americans called Africans* (1833) was the first anti-slavery book published in the United States. She ably defended John Brown's exploit at Harper's Ferry. In this connection mention should also be made of the *Appeal* of David Walker, a Negro of Boston, which appeared in 1829. This work was addressed to the slaves, being a recital of their wrongs and a protest against proscription. Its incendiary tone created great excitement in the South, the governors of Georgia and Virginia sending to their legislatures special messages about it. Representative of the more conservative anti-slavery sentiment was William Ellery Channing, the New England idealist and scholar, advanced Unitarian and social reformer. In 1835 he published his *Slavery*, which with lofty spirit showed that the institution was out of harmony with the upward movement of humanity. In restraint and pose, in logic and diction, the little book is classic.

44. Southern Sentiment against Slavery.—While no one in the South took such radical ground against slavery as the Abolitionists (except here and there perhaps a character like the sturdy and independent Cassius Clay of Kentucky), there were many individuals in this section who for one reason or another desired to be relieved of the system of slavery. We have seen that in the Revolutionary War the sentiment of many representative patriots was opposed to slavery, and that as early as 1778 Virginia attempted to abolish it. The efforts in this state were most prolonged, new attempts being made as late as 1829 and 1831–2. These would have succeeded if it had not been for the state's unfair system of representation, of which Jefferson so frequently complained. From some petitions of 1776 to the Constitutional Convention in the state, it is to be seen that North Carolina also made efforts in the same direction, renewing in 1835 her attempt for gradual abolition. Here, however, as in Virginia, the "interests," represented by the large owners and planters, had never allowed to the anti-slavery people fair representation. In South Carolina the "up-country" was likewise opposed to slavery; but the subject did not succeed in getting a real hearing until after 1808. In 1819, Hayne leading the reform, it was only by a majority of 3 in the Senate that the state decided not to prohibit the importation of slaves from other states. It seems that the Charleston capitalists, with Hayne as their spokesman, desired to check importation for two reasons, one to make their own slave property more valuable, and the other to start in South Carolina other industries than cotton and rice production. However selfish the motive, such a movement would have had beneficent results, and other men as well as Hayne realized the benefits that would accrue to South Carolina from a well-grounded industrialism. Generally it was the Scotch-Irish people in the "up-country" of the state who favored the overthrow of slavery in order that they might control their states as well as because many of them actually opposed slavery on moral grounds. It was this "up-country" element in Virginia (then largely in what is now West Virginia) that fought and largely won the Revolution, and that thus had much reason to control the state.

45. State Rights.—While, however, there was some sentiment in the South for the freedom of the slaves or the amelioration of their condition, more and more the dominant thought in this section became crystallized in what was known as the doctrine of State Rights. This term designates those rights of government and administration which a state that has become a member of a federal union may still exercise, and within the sphere of whose activity the central government may not legally intrude. It was claimed by the advocates of the principle that while the federal government was given specific powers by the Constitution, each state retained exclusive control of matters relating to the everyday life of its people. Calhoun was the foremost expounder of the view, and the theories of Nullification and Secession were based upon it.

46. Liberia.—It is now time to record the progress of an attempt by some enlightened Americans to solve the problem of the free Negro, who labored under so many disabilities. As early as 1787 Sierra Leone in Africa had been founded by the English as a colony for free Negroes, some of whom had gained their freedom in consequence of Lord Mansfield's decision in 1772, more of whom had been discharged from the British army after the American Revolution, and all of whom were leading in England a more or less precarious existence. In 1787 about four hundred were taken to a district purchased from the king of Sierra Leone, and five years later twelve hundred Negroes who had escaped from the United States to Canada were also taken thither. England cared with wisdom for the Negroes, giving them a daily allowance for the first six months, then assigning lands to them, and generally seeking to bring them under the influence of religious education. As early as 1783 it had been proposed that such a colony as this should be established for free American Negroes; but it was not until 1816 that the American Colonization Society was formed, and not until 1822, after a treaty with certain native princes had been concluded, that active settlement began under the direction of the heroic Josiah Ashmun, each man being allotted a tract of thirty acres with the means of cultivating it. After a while, however, the agents of the society became discouraged at the difficulties that had to be overcome and returned to America with a few faint-hearted colonists. Others rallied around a spirited and determined Negro, Elijah Johnson, and remained, enlarging the colony by the purchase of new tracts of land. The trials were many, but in spite of deprivations, dissensions, and the threatening attitude of native chiefs, Liberia continued to exist. In 1847 the country was officially left to its own resources, becoming an independent republic. In 1833, in his pamphlet entitled *Thoughts on African Colonization*, Garrison showed the futility of the whole plan as a means of solving the problem of slavery in the United States; and time has justified his view, for Liberia has had no abiding influence on the position of the Negro in America.

47. Abolition Abroad.—While this experiment was still in its early stage, and while the Abolitionists were just forming their organizations, news came in 1833 that at last England had freed her slaves. This

she had done in a typically English way, paying
£20,000,000 to the slave-owners in her dominions and
keeping the slaves under a system of apprenticeship
for a term of years. Garrison now brought an English
orator to America, and generally the achievement
excited interest. It is well to observe the progress of
abolition in other countries also. Denmark in 1792
had been the first European power to abolish the
slave-trade. Sweden abolished the traffic in 1813,
Holland abolished the trade in 1814 and slavery itself
in her colonies in 1846, and Portugal formally forbade
the trade in 1836. The experience of France in Santo
Domingo has already been sketched. In 1818 the
abolition of the slave-trade was effectually accomplished in this colony, and the independence of the
island was formally recognized by France in 1825.
The South American countries generally abolished
slavery as they emancipated themselves from Spain.
Throughout this period, however, in spite of all these
efforts for reform, there was an illicit slave-traffic on
the high seas, and overtures for an international right
of search were constantly made between the great
nations. These efforts did not really succeed until
Abraham Lincoln became president of the United
States. In 1860 the three representative systems of
slavery in the New World were those in the United
States, in Cuba, and in Brazil.

48. Annexation of Texas.—In 1821 Mexico revolted from Spain. At first she tried an imperial form
of government, but in 1824 became a federal republic.
Texas, then a part of Mexico, was joined with two
other provinces into a state. Here American immigration increased so rapidly that Mexico, becoming
alarmed, established military rule and passed antislavery laws. Texas revolted, and an attempt to
reduce her to submission resulted in her gaining her
independence in 1836 under the lead of General Sam
Houston. Independence was followed by a desire
for annexation to the United States; but the North
feared such an addition to slave territory. In 1844
the question was the leading one in the presidential
election, and James K. Polk came into office on a
platform pledged to annexation. The Mexican War
which followed, growing out of a dispute between
Mexico and Texas with reference to the boundary
line, was generally regarded in the North as a contest
waged in behalf of slavery, and it did much to embitter
the sections against each other.

49. Compromise of 1850. Fugitive Slave Law.—
Various new matters now demanded legislation. The
fact that some Northern people assisted slaves to escape was generally obnoxious to Southern minds.
Moreover, aside from Texas, other territory in the
Southwest had been acquired for the nation by the

Mexican War. The North, by a bill known as the Wilmot Proviso, sought to enact that slavery should be prohibited in this territory; and the South contended that it should be free from federal interference. Moreover, California, that had grown up all in a year as a result of the discovery of gold, was now seeking admission as a free state, without even having been a regularly organized territory. Accordingly, early in 1850 Henry Clay introduced in the Senate some new compromise resolutions. These resulted in two bills whose provisions, as finally agreed on, were in substance as follows: (1) California was to be admitted as a free state; (2) Utah and New Mexico were to be organized as territories with no provision as to slavery; (3) the boundaries of Texas were to be fixed substantially as they are at present, and $10,000,000 was to be paid this state for her relinquishment of boundary claims on the nation for the payment of her public debt; (4) the slave-trade was to be prohibited in the District of Columbia; and (5) a new and stringent fugitive slave law was to be passed. Both political parties professed to be satisfied, and Henry Clay once more went home beguiled by the fancy that he had saved the Union. Neither side, however, was really satisfied, and the whole issue was to be brought forth again only four years later by the trouble in Kansas. The North was especially angered by the Fugitive

Slave Law. Gradually the states in that section had succeeded in obstructing the execution of the act of 1793, and in 1842 Pennsylvania by a case at court definitely decided that her state officials could not be compelled to aid in the return of runaway slaves. The new law made possible many gross abuses. It provided for the appointment in each county of a federal commissioner who was to decide without a jury upon the identity of each fugitive brought before him. He was in no case to accept the word of the fugitive, and when he returned a man he was to receive for his fee twice as much money as when he did not return one. The writ for a return moreover was to be executed by United States marshals upon whom a heavy penalty was visited if a slave escaped. Any person could be called to the assistance of a marshal, and anyone who assisted a fugitive was to be heavily punished. All of this was too much for the Northern states, which began to make the act of no effect. In the interval 1854-60 (these dates inclusive) nine states passed what were known as Personal Liberty Laws. These generally forbade state officers to assist in the return of alleged fugitives; secured counsel for the fugitives, who were also to have the benefit of *habeas corpus* and trial by jury; prohibited the use of state jails for the detention of supposed runaways; and imposed a heavy penalty for the seizure of any free person.

50. The Underground Railroad.—"The Underground Railroad" was the name given to the various means by which those in the North who opposed slavery assisted fugitives in escaping from their masters and in finding their way to places of safety. By the system thousands of persons were enabled to get to Canada beyond the reach of the Fugitive Slave Law. The most favored routes were through Ohio and Pennsylvania. At various places there were "stations," generally private houses where the slaves were kept and fed in garrets or cellars during the day, being sent on their way when night came. The work was done at great personal risk, as it was done in defiance of the law and as Southern legislatures offered large rewards for the delivery of assistants caught south of the Mason and Dixon's line. The magnitude of the operations may be seen from the fact that for years before the Civil War about 500 Negroes annually made trips from Canada to the South to assist their friends in escaping. One Negro woman, Harriet Tubman, who had escaped from Maryland, made nineteen journeys into the South and brought away about 300 slaves. Many Northern people suffered in the cause. Levi Coffin, a Quaker of Newport, Ind., was commonly considered the head of the enterprise. Once being asked under oath before a grand jury if he had aided slaves, he replied that he had no legal knowledge of having done so. He had ministered, he said, to certain destitute persons who told him that they had been slaves; but he had only their word for it, and as the word of a slave could not be received in court, he could not reasonably be considered guilty. He was released. Everybody did not fare so well, however. Ruth Shore, of Sandusky, O., paid in fines for assisting runaway slaves a total of $3,000. Thomas Garrett paid $8,000, and Calvin Fairbank served seventeen years in the penitentiary for his work in the cause. In spite of legal pressure, however, the work went on. The investigator of the subject * names 3,211 "agents, station keepers, and conductors." Coffin received annually in his house about 100 fugitives, and Garrett helped altogether as many as 2,700 to escape.

51. Renewal of the Slave-Trade.—We have seen that the first national act against the slave-trade was passed in 1794 and that the traffic was nominally abolished in 1807. The measure of the latter year was lacking from the first in any adequate machinery for its enforcement, and before long the national government became aware that an illicit trade was still being carried on. Through such narrow inlets as those near the ports of Galveston and Fernandina, slaves were smuggled in, sometimes in great numbers.

* Siebert.

From 1820 to 1840, largely as the result of a repressive measure of 1819, the traffic declined greatly. On account of the great development of the cotton industry, however, there grew up in the Southern states after 1820 a great demand for more land and more slaves. The desire for land accounted for the annexation of Texas, and that for more slaves was at first satisfied for the most part by importations from Virginia and Maryland, which states now became joined to the far South by the closest ties of interest. Thus matters drifted until 1850, between which date and 1860 there was so much friction between the North and the South and such an increase in the value of slave labor that the controlling opinion of the South was but voiced in a resolution offered in a commercial convention in Vicksburg in 1859 to the effect that "all laws, State or Federal, prohibiting the African slave-trade, ought to be repealed." In the decade just mentioned there was such a remarkable increase of illicit traffic and actual importations that the movement may almost be termed a re-opening of the slave-trade.* The traffic became more and more open and defiant until, as Stephen A. Douglas computed, as many as 15,000 slaves were brought into the country in 1859. It was not until the Lincoln government in 1862 hanged the first trader who ever

---

* DuBois, *Suppression of the Slave-Trade*, 178.

suffered the extreme penalty of the law, and made with Great Britain a treaty embodying the principle of international right of search, that the trade was effectually checked. By the end of the war it was entirely suppressed, though as late as 1866 a squadron of ships patrolled the slave coast.

52. Kansas-Nebraska Bill.—The point of the Kansas-Nebraska Bill of 1854 is very simple, this measure being merely a repealing of the provisions of the Missouri Compromise in the interest of the slave power. It was largely the act of Stephen A. Douglas, chairman of the Senate Committee on Territories, who contended that the Compromise of 1850 had in giving territories the right of option as to slavery annulled the Missouri Compromise. This construction was embodied in a bill for the organization of the territories of Kansas and Nebraska with limits much larger than those of the present states of Kansas and Nebraska. It provided for "squatter sovereignty," that is, that the people in any territory should be free to form and regulate their domestic institutions in their own way, subject only to the Constitution of the United States. The North felt that it was outraged by the bill, and immediately the Republican party began to be formed.

53. The Anthony Burns Incident.—It was not long before public sentiment began to make itself felt, and the first demonstration took place in Boston. Anthony Burns was a slave who escaped from Virginia and made his way to Boston, where he was at work in the winter of 1853-4. He was discovered by a United States marshal who presented a writ for his arrest just at the time of the repeal of the Missouri Compromise in May, 1854. Public feeling became greatly aroused. Wendell Phillips and Theodore Parker delivered strong addresses at a meeting in Faneuil Hall while an unsuccessful attempt to rescue Burns from the Court House was made under the leadership of Thomas W. Higginson, who, with others of the attacking party, was wounded. It was finally decided in court that Burns must be returned to his master. The law was obeyed; but Boston had been made very angry, and generally her feeling had counted for something in the history of the country. The people draped their houses in mourning and hissed the procession that took Burns to his ship. At the wharf a riot was averted only by a minister's call to prayer. This incident did more to crystallize Northern sentiment against slavery than any other except the exploit of John Brown, and this was the last time that a fugitive slave was taken out of Boston. Burns himself was afterwards bought from his master by popular subscription. He became a free citizen of Boston, and ultimately a Baptist minister in Canada.

54. Dred Scott Decision.—One further act was yet to fill the cup of the North to the brim. In 1834 Dr. Emerson, an army officer stationed in Missouri, removed to Illinois, taking with him his slave, Dred Scott. Two years later, again accompanied by Scott, he went to Minnesota. In Illinois slavery was prohibited by state law and Minnesota was a free territory. In 1838 Emerson returned with Scott to Missouri. After a while the slave raised the important question, Had not his residence outside of a slave state made him a free man? Beaten by his master in 1848, with the aid of anti-slavery lawyers Scott brought a suit against him for assault and battery, the circuit court of St. Louis rendering a decision in his favor. Emerson appealed and in 1852 the Supreme Court of the State reversed the decision of the lower court. Not long after this Emerson sold Scott to a citizen of New York named Sandford. Scott now brought suit against Sandford, on the ground that they were citizens of different states. The case finally reached the Supreme Court of the United States, which in 1857 handed down the decision that Scott was not a citizen of Missouri and had no standing in the federal courts, that a slave was only a piece of property, and that a master might take his property to any place he chose within the jurisdiction of the United States. The ownership of Scott and his family soon passed

to a Massachusetts family by whom they were lib-
crated; but the important decision that his case had
called forth aroused the most intense excitement
throughout the country.

55. " Uncle Tom's Cabin."—In the year 1852 appeared a book that had an amazing sale and that
stirred the heart of the country on the subject of
slavery as it had never been moved before. For some
years before the Compromise of 1850 Harriet Beecher
Stowe, wife of a theological professor, had been living
with her husband in Cincinnati. There she was close
to the system of slavery and saw much of its actual
working. In 1850 Professor Stowe accepted a position
in Bowdoin College, Brunswick, Me., and removed
his family thither. Here in the form of a story with
the title *Uncle Tom's Cabin*, Mrs. Stowe brought together her observations on slavery, first as a serial
and then as a book. What the work lacked in literary
finish, it more than made up in living interest. Its
characters represented strongly the different types
of people living in the South. Here was Uncle Tom
himself, embodiment of all that was pious in the
Negro nature; behind him a long line of plantation
Negroes. Here were little Eva, a spirit of light in the
sad world around her; her father, the over-indulgent
and improvident master; Aunt Ophelia from New
England, to whom the whole South was "shiftless";

Cassy, the slave darling fallen on evil days; Simon Legree, the worst type of plantation slave-owner; and George Harris, the ambitious spirit longing to break its bonds. The book was avowedly a novel of purpose, and many people have criticised it as overdrawn. No work, however, that attempts to set forth a great moral wrong can be truly overdrawn, for actual suffering is always greater than any portrayal of it. At any rate the South felt itself misrepresented; so that in 1853 Mrs. Stowe published *A Key to Uncle Tom's Cabin*, setting forth the documents and facts used in the story, and showing, among other things, that the prototype of Uncle Tom was Josiah Henson, a Negro who, born a slave in Maryland, escaped to Canada in 1828, became a lecturer in the United States, and on the last of three trips to England was entertained by Queen Victoria at Windsor Castle. Mrs. Stowe wrote a great many other books; but, with the exception of *Dred*, a book ominous with the note of impending disaster, they all pale into insignificance by the side of her great success. *Uncle Tom's Cabin*, however, was alone strong enough for a life-work, and even to-day it receives frequent presentations on the stage.

56. **Henry Ward Beecher.**—Of only less service to the cause of the slave than Mrs. Stowe was her brother, Henry Ward Beecher. This remarkable preacher, by his bold support of reforms, made his

large and intelligent congregation at Plymouth Church, Brooklyn, one of the most famous in the world. He was untiring in his support of the anti-slavery cause and on one occasion appealed to his audience by bringing a slave girl into his pulpit. His greatest achievement perhaps was a series of speeches in England in 1863 in the delivery of which he was constantly hissed. As the cotton manufacturing industry of England was dependent on the supply from the cotton states, opinion in that country with reference to the Civil War in America was not all on the side of the North; and Beecher did much to win favor for the side of the Union.

57. Charles Sumner.—What Beecher was in the pulpit Charles Sumner was in the United States Senate. This distinguished and scholarly statesman came into prominence in 1845 by a Fourth of July oration denouncing war. In 1851 he was sent to the Senate, of which he was a member until his death in 1874. Though not an Abolitionist, he became the leader of the anti-slavery forces, and by his bitter invective and unflinching opposition to the Compromise of 1850 and the Kansas-Nebraska Bill he incurred the intense hatred of the South, receiving many threats of personal violence. In 1856 in fact, while writing at his desk in the senate chamber, he was severely assaulted with a cane by Preston S. Brooks of South Carolina. The attack greatly embittered the North. Sumner himself was forced to retire temporarily from public life, and never fully recovered. As early as 1864 he formulated what was known as the "State Suicide" theory with reference to the seceded states, and he became the leader of the opposition to President Johnson's plan of reconstruction. It was due to him more than to any other man that the principle of suffrage, irrespective of race or color, became fixed and universal in the American system.

58. John Brown.—For forty years slavery had been the most important subject before the American people. Garrison had been persecuted, Lovejoy had been killed, Phillips and Douglass had talked, slaves had escaped to Canada, and Mrs. Stowe had written a book; and still slavery had gone on its masterful career, seemingly invincible. At length, however, the tension had reached the point where only a spark was needed to send the country into flame. That spark was supplied by John Brown. This man was born in Connecticut in 1800. In his earlier years he made various experiments in business, in all of which he was unsuccessful. After living for years a very unsettled life, in 1855 he joined five of his sons in Kansas, where the opponents and the advocates of slavery were fiercely arrayed against each other. Here, as Wendell Phillips said, he actually began life. He became the leader of the radical anti-slavery men, and on May 24, 1856, he massacred five of his opponents at Pottawatomie. Later in the year, at Ossawatomie, he attracted national attention by the energy with which he repelled a strong invading force from Missouri. All of this was merely the execution of his conviction that as slavery was an unholy cause he was justified in killing slaveholders. The really notable deed of his life occurred in 1859. He conceived a plan to seize, with the aid of an armed force, some strong position in the mountains of Virginia, whence he might sally forth and make the slave power generally insecure. In pursuance of his plan, as a blind he engaged a farm near his objective point, and on October 16, 1859, with nineteen assistants, five of whom were Negroes, he surprised and captured the arsenal at Harper's Ferry. Two days later, after being wounded, he was captured by United States troops under the command of Robert E. Lee. He was convicted of treason and murder, and hanged December 2nd. John Brown's exploit made a profound impression on the country, and he has since been the subject of most conflicting opinion. Some people think of him as a fanatic who committed a criminal deed, while to others he was a man of noble purpose borne by the intensity of his convictions into martyrdom.

CHAPTER VI

NEGRO EFFORT FOR FREEDOM AND CULTURE

59. Strivings of the Slave.—To the Negro in bonds the institution of slavery was one long night with little hope of day. His highest impulses, his tenderest emotions, his every incentive to high endeavor, felt the blasting effects of the system. He might work in the field from sunrise to sunset; but none of the fruit of his labor was his own. He might cherish the tenderest sentiments of a father, only to see his child torn from his arms forever. He might possess lofty ambition or distinctive genius, and find effort made to deprive him of every quality of manhood. With his brethren he sang in the night-time his wild "sorrow song," "I've been a-listenin' all the night long;" and in yearning for the joys of heaven he prayed for deliverance from physical bondage. To escape at once from slavery, however, was possible only by regular manumission, by open revolt, or by running away. It is the purpose of this chapter to review some of the efforts put forth by Negroes themselves to cast off the chains that bound them and to advance in education and culture.

60. Fugitives.—In spite of the harsh laws against fugitives and the certain trail of bloodhounds, a great many slaves elected to run away. The attempt was commonly to direct one's way to the North, where the fugitive slave law of 1793 was not generally in force. Traveling largely by night under the guidance of the north star, the Negroes sustained themselves as best they could. The Dismal Swamp in Virginia became a famous hiding-place. A colony here defied owners right in the midst of a strong slavery community. Soldiers never ventured into the colony, and bloodhounds sent thither did not return. As many of the slaves made their way into Canada, an attempt was made in 1828 to effect some arrangement with Great Britain for the return of those who escaped thither; but this failed. In the far South, while Florida was still under Spanish rule, there was some movement in the opposite direction, many fugitives taking refuge and intermarrying with the Indians. In 1816 American troops blew up a fort on the Appalachicola that was the headquarters of many slaves who had run away; and the first Seminole War was very largely caused by fugitives. When Florida was annexed slave-hunting increased, and then the escaping Negroes made their way as far south as the Everglades. The second Seminole War was even more directly caused by fugitives than the first. The famous chief-

tain Osceola had a wife who was the daughter of a
Negro woman who had found refuge with the Indians.
This woman (the wife) was seized in 1835 while at
Fort King, being claimed as a slave by her mother's
former owner. Osceola vowed revenge, and was
temporarily imprisoned. On being released he conducted the war with remarkable bravery and resource,
and it stands to the eternal shame of American arms
that he was captured under a flag of truce.

61. Insurrections.—It always happens when one
race is in subjection to another that among those
in power there is constant fear of an uprising. This
fact accounts for much of the harshness of the slave
codes and for the attempts to check importations
of Negroes. On plantations patrolmen frequently
searched the quarters for concealed weapons. All
told, however, the insurrections of slaves in America
were very few in number. In 1687 there was in Virginia a conspiracy among the blacks in the Northern
Neck that was detected just in time to prevent
slaughter; and in Surry County in 1710 there was a
similar plot, betrayed by one of the conspirators.
The attempt in New York in 1712 resulted in the
execution of many Negroes. In 1740 some slaves on
the coast of South Carolina, under the lead of one of
their number named Cato, began an indiscriminate
slaughter of the whites in which many lives were lost.

The news came to Wilton while the people were in church, and the Negroes were soon overtaken in a large field celebrating their achievement with draughts of rum. They were dispersed and their leaders hanged. More ambitious in plan than this attempt was the effort made in Richmond in 1800 and known as Gabriel's Insurrection. This attempt "was planned by two young and intelligent negroes; Gabriel, a slave, twenty-four years old, and one Jack Bowler, aged twenty-eight, neither of whom had an especial personal grievance to inspire him. They organized as many as 1,000 negroes in Henrico county, arming them with scythes and knives, and marched toward the city during the night. Forced to halt by a stream swollen and impassable from a recent storm, they disbanded, expecting to renew the attempt on the following night. . . . Their plot was disclosed by a slave Pharaoh, who had escaped from them and aroused the citizens of Richmond before the attack could be made. A reward of $300 was offered for the leaders, Gabriel and Jack. They were caught and executed, but a large number of the conspirators were mercifully acquitted or the charges against them were dismissed on account of lack of evidence. This plot resulted in the institution of a public guard for the city, of 68 persons under a captain and other officers."*

* Ballagh, *Slavery in Virginia*, 92.

62. Denmark Vesey.—Two of the insurrections of Negroes deserve greater consideration than the others, one because of the ambitiousness of its plan and the other because of its actual achievement. The first was conceived by Denmark Vesey. This man was probably born in Saint Thomas, West Indies, in 1767; but the first fourteen years of his life are a blank. He is first seen in 1781 as one of three hundred and ninety Negroes being transported to Santo Domingo on board a vessel commanded by one Captain Vesey. He did not remain there, however, being subsequently taken by Captain Vesey to Charleston, S. C. For nearly twenty years he was the faithful servant of this man, who in course of time retired from his iniquitous profession. In 1800, at the age of thirty-three, by winning a prize in a lottery Denmark Vesey found himself in possession of $1,500. Of this amount he paid $600 for his liberty. He worked at his trade, carpentry, amassed some wealth, and won general esteem. He was fluent in French as well as English, and being gifted with remarkable personal magnetism, by his intelligence and sagacity he inspired among the slaves of the city a respect that amounted almost to veneration. He became the father of several children, but no one of these could he call his own, as under the slave code a child followed the condition of the mother. In course of time Vesey conceived a plan that contemplated nothing less than the total annihilation of the white population of Charleston. For years he sowed among his brethren the seeds of discontent, and such was his discreetness that although he played in every possible way upon the superstitions of the Negroes, and interpreted any public event as pointing to liberty, at no time did he come under suspicion. At length the time for action came. Vesey joined to himself five associates, Peter Poyas, Rolla Bennett, Ned Bennett, Monday Gell, and Gullah Jack. Aided by these men he brought into his plan thousands of Negroes in the city of Charleston and in the outlying districts, upon whom all the while the greatest secrecy and regular attention to daily tasks were enjoined. He finally selected the midnight of Sunday, July 22, 1822, as the time for his attack upon the city, Sunday because on that day many Negroes from the plantations were in Charleston, and July because in midsummer many of the white people were away at the summer resorts. Of one class of slaves he had a peculiar distrust. "Take care," said he, "and don't mention the plan to those waiting men who receive presents of old coats, etc., from their masters, or they'll betray us." That his suspicions were justified was abundantly proved by the sequel. Late in May one of those very "waiting men" endeavored to inform against him; but so insufficient was the knowledge of this man that Peter Poyas and Mingo Harth, one of the minor leaders, who had been arrested, were released. Ned Bennett, who also came under suspicion, committed the daring deed of voluntarily going before the authorities with the request to be examined, outwitting them by his coolness and throwing the city into greater tumult than ever. The original plan was now hastened by four weeks, Sunday, June 16, being the new date. Again in a few days it was divulged by a "waiting man," who in this instance had more accurate knowledge than the first informant. The attempt to carry out the plan was easily suppressed, and the leaders were tried before a special court in which appeared Robert Y. Hayne, then just rising into great distinction. Vesey conducted his case with great skill, but he was finally condemned to death. With Spartan courage Peter Poyas said to his associates, "Do not open your lips! Die silent as you shall see me die." In all, thirty-five men were executed and thirty-seven banished. Thus closed the insurrection that for the magnitude of its plan, the care with which it was matured, and the faithfulness of the leaders to one another, was never equalled by a similar attempt for freedom in the United States.*

63. Nat Turner.—The other important insurrection was that of Nat Turner, a religious enthusiast and the

---

* See Grimké, the main source for the paragraph.

type of the emotional insurrectionist as Vesey was of the intellectual. This man was born in 1800 in Southampton County, Virginia. He was unusually precocious, learning to read with such rapidity that he came to be regarded as a prodigy. From his childhood he believed that he was divinely chosen for some great mission, claiming to hear voices and to see visions, among others a vision of white and black spirits in battle. In course of time he became convinced that his mission was to deliver his people. An eclipse in February, 1831, was accepted as the sign for which he had been waiting; but nothing was done until after a peculiar appearance of the sun on August 13th. With four friends, Sam Edwards, Henry Porter, Nelson Williams, and Hark Travis, he set about the work, being joined very soon by a gigantic and athletic Negro named Will. The insurrectionists ultimately numbered fifty or sixty. Their weapons were most indiscriminate, knives and axes as well as guns. On Sunday night, August 21, near Cross Keys, Turner and his associates began their work by killing five members of his master's family. Throughout the night they went on with the work, killing any white person in the neighborhood. Next morning they killed all the pupils in a schoolhouse. In all, fifty-seven white people were killed; others would have died if their slaves had not defended them. By noon the news had spread. United States troops from Fortress Monroe came to the scene of action; also the militia from various counties in Virginia and North Carolina. The insurrectionists were hunted like wild beasts. After Turner had succeeded in concealing himself for six weeks, he was finally discovered, tried, convicted, and hanged, as were sixteen of his associates. As he predicted, the day of his death was one of terrible thunder and lightning. The insurrection naturally created the wildest fear and excitement throughout the South. Its effects upon legislation were immediate, the slave codes being made more harsh.*

64. The Amistad Incident.—Once while one hundred and thirty-five slaves were being taken from Virginia to New Orleans, Madison Washington, one of the number, organized a rebellion and took possession of the vessel, carrying it to Nassau, an English port, where the authorities refused to surrender the Negroes. An incident very similar to this, but more famous and more important because of its legal consequences, was that of the Spanish slave schooner, *L'Amistad*, bound in 1839 for Puerto Principe, Cuba. The fifty-four slaves on board were just from Africa,

---

* The exhaustive study of Nat Turner is a Johns Hopkins dissertation, Drewry's *The Southampton Insurrection*. It is a pity that a work that brings together so many facts should be marred by a partisan tone.

where they had been kidnapped. Under the lead of one of their number, Joseph Cinquez, an African prince who had become disgusted at the cruel treatment accorded him and his companions, they revolted and took possession of the vessel. They killed two of the crew, most of the others escaping. They then commanded their owners, two white men whose lives they had spared, to steer them back to Africa. These men made a pretense of so doing, but really steered north. After considerable wandering the vessel was captured off Long Island by the United States brig *Washington*, under the command of Lieutenant Gedney, and taken into the harbor of New London, Conn. The Negroes were bound over to await trial as pirates. The Spanish minister, Calderon, demanded that the Negroes be surrendered as "property rescued from pirates," and President Van Buren was disposed to yield to the demand in accordance with a treaty with Spain. The suggestion, however, met with the most violent opposition from the anti-slavery element. The trial lasted for some months, and in this time friends taught the Africans to read so that they could tell their story without the aid of an interpreter. The United States Circuit Court finally decided that inasmuch as the international slave-trade was illegal even by Spanish law, the Negroes were free men and had been justified in obtaining their liberty by force.

The decision was sustained in March, 1841, by the United States Supreme Court, before which John Quincy Adams appeared in behalf of the Negroes. Lewis Tappan, one of the organizers of the New York Anti-Slavery Society, now raised among friends of the cause money for the transportation of the Negroes back to Africa. In the company of missionaries they were sent to Sierra Leone whence Great Britain had them taken to their own homes.

65. Story of a Representative Negro.—Perhaps no case that could be cited better illustrates the strivings of the quiet, thrifty, conservative Negro under the system of slavery than that of Lunsford Lane. This man was a slave belonging to a citizen of Raleigh, N. C., and grew up before the era of unusual harshness to slaves which came after the Nat Turner insurrection of 1831. At an early age he learned to read and write, and he gathered much general information from the conversation of his master's guests and from the political speeches of Calhoun and other statesmen. He once heard a distinguished minister say, "It is impossible to enslave an intelligent people;" and he never forgot these words. Earnestly desirous of his freedom, he carefully hoarded the fees given him by friends of his master, and by the time he had grown to manhood he had saved several hundred dollars. A part of this money Lane lost in bad investments, and some he spent in special care for his wife, the slave of another master, one Mr. Smith. By his father he had been taught the secret of making a superior kind of smoking tobacco, and he now began to manufacture the product for market, hiring his time from his master for from $100 to $120 a year. The master dying after a few years, he undertook to purchase his freedom from his mistress, the price agreed upon being $1,000. As a slave, however, he could not make a contract; hence he entrusted the matter to his wife's master. Smith, after making the purchase, asked court's leave to emancipate Lane. By law, however, a slave could be freed for meritorious service only. The best thing then that Smith could do was to take Lane with him to New York on his next business trip, and have the freedom papers issued there. After this process Lane returned to Raleigh, where his business expanded generally, as among other things he manufactured pipes and kept a store. He now undertook to buy his wife and six children. Smith insisted on notes to the amount of $2,500, although eight years before he had bought the wife and two children for only $560. All this time Lane was very modest in his attitude toward the white people, dressing as poorly as when a slave, and doing or saying nothing that could cause him to be considered an agitator. All the same there were those who were jealous of his pros-

perity, and these called to mind an almost forgotten
act that forbade free Negroes from other states to
come to North Carolina. Lane was forced to leave.
He returned after a short while, however, to straighten
up his business. He had paid Smith $560 in cash,
and had taken one of his boys to New York. He gave
his house and lot for $500, undertaking to pay in cash
the balance of $1,440. By lecturing in the North,
within one year he raised the amount he wished.
Lane now asked of the governor of North Carolina
permission to return to the state. The governor replied that he had no authority to grant such permission, but that under the law he thought it would be
all right for Lane to return, provided he did not remain
longer than twenty days. Lane got back to Raleigh
Saturday, April 23, 1842. He spent Sunday with his
family, and on Monday went to Smith's store to finish
up his business. He was arrested and accused of
"delivering abolition lectures in the State of Massachusetts." In court he recounted with simple pathos
the whole story of his life, and as the matter was
clearly outside of the jurisdiction of a North Carolina
court, the case was dismissed. The court house was
surrounded by a mob, however, Lane's trunk was
searched for abolition literature, and he himself was
subjected to other indignities. He was put in jail
for safe keeping, and spent the night at the home of

an honored citizen. Early the next morning, however, he was tarred and feathered. The soldiery came at last to his protection, and the next day he set out with his family for Philadelphia. Several friends now assisted him, giving him food for the journey and arranging to have him take the train on the edge of the town in order to avoid a mob at the station. Lane's later life was spent in Boston, Oberlin, and Worcester. He had some success in selling a medicine which he made, and he was active in the abolition movement until his death.*

66. Free Negroes.—A matter frequently lost sight of in the consideration of the larger aspects of slavery is that of the free person of color. Free Negroes were much more numerous than is sometimes thought, and contributed a corresponding influence to society as a whole. They formed really one-ninth of the total Negro population of the country, there being in 1860, 487,970 free persons to 3,953,760 slaves. Except in such centers as New Orleans and Charleston, most of these people were looked upon as forming a vicious and indolent element, from which society had more to fear than from any other class. All sorts of restrictive laws were enacted; but these were not generally enforced, and over half of the free Negroes in the country resided in the South. Although they

* Bassett, *Anti-Slavery Leaders*, 60–74.

labored under many disabilities, they engaged in almost every occupation that Negroes pursue to-day. A visitor from England received the impression in Washington and other cities that they enjoyed a special monopoly of the barber's trade. Their economic life left most to be desired in the nonslaveholding states. Even here, however, some found a place in domestic service, and a few made a beginning in the professions. "Their general status, taken as a whole, was better in Louisiana than anywhere else in the country, North or South. In 1836, in the city of New Orleans, 855 free people of color paid taxes on property assessed at $2,462,470, and owned 620 slaves. In 1860 the property holdings of the same class for the state at large were estimated at from $13,000,000 to $15,000,000. There were free colored planters in Louisiana whose property in land and slaves was valued at from $25,000 to $150,000. Many of these people enjoyed educational advantages and lived amidst refined surroundings equal to any possessed by their white neighbors. . . . What was true of conditions in New Orleans and Louisiana was also true of Baltimore, Charleston, Mobile, and other less important 'free negro' centers in the South, and of Philadelphia, New York, and other places in the North." *

* Stone, *The Negro in the South.*

67. Education before the Civil War.—The first schools for Negroes were private ones, such as everywhere preceded public schools. In 1704 one such school was opened in New York, in 1770 one in Philadelphia, and in 1798 one in Boston.* In certain places in what is now the Middle West private schools became largely supported by manumitted Negroes. In the South efforts were of course more sporadic; but deserving of attention is the education which Negroes received through private or clandestine sources. More than one slave learned the alphabet while entertaining the son of his master. As early as 1764 the editor of a paper in Williamsburg, Va., had established a school for Negroes; † and about 1800 a Negro, the Rev. John Chavis, passed "through a regular course of academic studies" at Washington Academy, now Washington and Lee University.‡ In Charleston for a long time before the Civil War free Negroes could attend schools especially designed for their benefit and kept by white people or other Negroes. The course of study not infrequently embraced such subjects as physiology, elementary physics, and plane geometry. After John Brown's raid the order went forth that no longer should any Negro teach Negroes. This resulted

---

* R. R. Wright, Jr., *Self-Help in Negro Education.*

† *William and Mary College Quarterly*, VI, 80.

‡ Ballagh, *Slavery in Virginia*, 110.

merely in a white person's being brought to sit in the classroom. On the outbreak of the Civil War, however, Negro schools were closed altogether. In the Northern states two institutions for the higher education of the Negro were established before the Civil War, Lincoln University in Pennsylvania in 1854 and Wilberforce in Ohio in 1856. Oberlin, moreover, was founded in 1833. One year later the trustees took the advanced ground of admitting Negro men and women on equal terms with white students. Though before this individual Negroes had found their way into Northern institutions, it was here at Oberlin that they first received a real welcome. In 1865 about one-third of the students were of the Negro race, and Oberlin still leads Northern colleges in the number of Negro graduates, especially women.

68. The Negro in the Public Eye.—In spite of the handicaps under which they labored, Negroes took an active part in the agitation preceding the Civil War. Mention has already been made of David Walker's *Appeal*. Samuel Ringgold Ward, author of *Autobiography of a Fugitive Negro*, was only one of several prominent Negro lecturers; and, as has been shown, one Negro woman, Harriet Tubman, took an unusually prominent part in the work of the Underground Railroad. Anything that indicated intellectual and moral capacity on the part of the Negro was eagerly seized upon by the opponents of slavery. Within four years the poems of Phillis Wheatley ran through three new editions; Elizabeth Greenfield, of Philadelphia, sang before the royalty of Europe; and Ira Aldridge achieved such success as a great tragedian that he was decorated by the emperors of Austria and Russia. The African Methodist Church was already demonstrating that the Negro could do something in organization; and everywhere individuals, by hardy effort, were showing forth the possibilities of the former slave in the estate of freedom.

69. Sojourner Truth.—Two Negroes, because of their unusual gifts, stood out with great prominence in the agitation. These were Sojourner Truth and Frederick Douglass. Sojourner Truth was born of slave parents about 1798 in Ulster County, New York. She remembered vividly in later years the cold, wet cellar-room in which slept the slaves of the family to which she belonged, and where she was taught by her mother to repeat the Lord's Prayer and to trust in God at all times. When in the course of gradual emancipation in New York she became legally free in 1827, her master refused to comply with the law. She left, but was pursued and found. Rather than have her go back, a friend paid for her services for the rest of the year. Then came an evening when, searching for one of her children that had been stolen and sold, she found herself a homeless wanderer. A Quaker family gave her lodging for the night. Subsequently she went to New York City, joined a Methodist church, and worked hard to improve her condition. Later, having decided to leave New York for a lecturing tour through the East, she made a small bundle of her belongings and informed a friend that her name was no longer *Isabella* but *Sojourner*. She went on her way, lecturing to people wherever she found them assembled and being entertained in many aristocratic homes. She was entirely untaught in the schools, but she was witty, original, and always suggestive. By her tact and her gift of song she kept down ridicule, and by her fervor and faith she won many friends for the anti-slavery cause. As to her name she said: "And the Lord gave me *Sojourner* because I was to travel up an' down the land showin' the people their sins an' bein' a sign unto them. Afterwards I told the Lord I wanted another name, 'cause everybody else had two names, an' the Lord gave me *Truth*, because I was to declare the truth to the people." *

70. Frederick Douglass.—Douglass was born in 1817 and lived for ten years as a slave upon a Maryland plantation. Then he was bought by a Baltimore shipbuilder. He learned to read, and, being attracted to *The Lady of the Lake*, when he escaped in 1838 and

* See Scruggs, 48–57.

went disguised as a sailor to New Bedford, Mass., he adopted the name *Douglas* (spelling it with two *s*'s however). He lived for several years in New Bedford, being assisted by Garrison in his efforts for an education. In 1841, at an anti-slavery convention in Nantucket, he exhibited such intelligence and showed himself the possessor of such a remarkable voice that he was made the agent of the Massachusetts Anti-Slavery Society. He now lectured extensively in England and the United States, and English friends raised £150 to enable him regularly to purchase his freedom. For a time he published a paper in Rochester. Later in life he became Recorder of Deeds in the District of Columbia, and then Minister to Hayti. At the time of his death in 1895 Douglass had won for himself a place of unique distinction. Large of heart and of mind, he was interested in every forward movement for his people; but his charity also embraced all men and all races. His reputation was national, and many of his speeches are to-day found in the standard books on the subject of oratory.

CHAPTER VII

EMANCIPATION

71. Steps Leading to the Proclamation.—For a long time Abraham Lincoln as President debated the advisability of issuing his proclamation emancipating the slaves in the Southern states, pressure from radical anti-slavery sources all the while being brought to bear upon him. He delayed until he was sure that the sentiment of his support was fully with him, and until he could act with grace to the Northern arms. After McClellan's unsuccessful campaign against Richmond, however, he felt that the freedom of the slaves was a military and a moral necessity for its effects upon both the North and the South; and Lee's defeat at Antietam, September 17, 1862, furnished the opportunity for which he had been waiting. Accordingly on September 22nd he issued a preliminary declaration giving notice that on January 1, 1863, he would free all slaves in the states still in rebellion, and asserting as before that the object of the war was the preservation of the Union.

72. Emancipation Proclamation.—The Proclamation as finally issued January 1st is one of the most important public documents in the history of the United States, ranking only below the Declaration of Independence and the Constitution itself. Its full text is as follows:—

Whereas, on the twenty-second day of September, in the year of our Lord one thousand eight hundred and sixty-two, a proclamation was issued by the President of the United States, containing among other things, the following, to-wit:

That on the first day of January, in the year of our Lord one thousand eight hundred and sixty-three, all persons held as slaves within any state or designated part of a state, the people whereof shall then be in rebellion against the United States, shall be then, thenceforward, and forever free; and the executive government of the United States, including the military and naval authority thereof, will recognize and maintain the freedom of such persons, and will do no act or acts to repress such persons, or any of them, in any efforts they may make for their actual freedom.

That the Executive will, on the first day of January aforesaid, by proclamation, designate the states and parts of states, if any, in which the people thereof shall then be in rebellion against the United States; and the fact that any state, or the people thereof, shall on that day be in good faith represented in the Congress of the United States, by members chosen thereto at elections wherein a majority of the qualified voters of such state shall have participated, shall, in the absence of strong countervailing testimony, be deemed conclusive evidence that such state, and the people thereof, are not then in rebellion against the United States.

Now, therefore, I, Abraham Lincoln, President of the United States, by virtue of the power in me vested as Commander-in-Chief of the Army and Navy of the United States, in time of actual armed rebellion against the authority and government of the United States, and as a fit and necessary war measure for suppressing said rebellion, do on this first day of January, in the year of our Lord one thousand eight hundred and sixty-three, and in accordance with my purpose so to do, publicly proclaimed for the full period of one hundred days from the date first above mentioned, order and designate as the states and parts of states wherein the people thereof respectively on this day are in rebellion against the United States, the following to-wit:

Arkansas, Texas, Louisiana (except the parishes of St. Bernard, Plaquemine, Jefferson, St. John, St. Charles, St. James, Ascension, Assumption, Terre Bonne, Lafourche, St. Marie, St. Martin, and Orleans, including the city of New Orleans), Mississippi, Alabama, Florida, Georgia, South Carolina, North Carolina, and Virginia (except the forty-eight counties designated as West Virginia, and also the counties of Berkeley, Accomac, Northampton, Elizabeth City, York, Princess Anne, and Norfolk, including the cities of Norfolk and Portsmouth), and which excepted parts are, for the present, left precisely as if this proclamation were not issued.

And by virtue of the power and for the purpose aforesaid, I do order and declare that all persons held as slaves within said designated states and parts of states are and henceforth shall be free, and that the executive government of the United States, including the military and naval authorities thereof, will recognize and maintain the freedom of said persons.

And I hereby enjoin upon the people so declared to be free to abstain from all violence, unless in necessary self-defense; and I recommend to them that, in all cases when allowed, they labor faithfully for reasonable wages.

And I further declare and make known that such persons, of suitable condition, will be received int« the armed service of the United States to garrison forts, positions, stations, and other places, and to man vessels of all sorts in said service.

And upon this act, sincerely believed to be an act of justice, warranted by the Constitution upon military necessity, I invoke the considerate judgment of mankind, and the gracious favor of Almighty God.

In testimony whereof, I have hereunto set my name, and caused the seal of the United States to be affixed.

Done at the City of Washington, this first day of January, in the year of our Lord one thousand eight hundred and sixty-three, and of the independence of the United States the eighty-seventh.

By the President,
ABRAHAM LINCOLN

WILLIAM H. SEWARD,
Secretary of State.

73. Effects of the Proclamation.—It is to be observed that the Proclamation was merely a war measure resting on the constitutional power of the President. Its effects on the legal status of the slaves

gave rise to much discussion; and it is to be noted that
it did not apply to what is now West Virginia, to seven
counties in Virginia, and to thirteen parishes in
Louisiana, which districts had already come under
federal jurisdiction. All questions raised by the
measure, however, were finally settled by the Thirteenth Amendment to the Constitution, and as a
matter of fact freedom actually followed the progress
of the American arms from 1863 to 1865. The moral
effect of the Proclamation was such as Lincoln had
foreseen, and the more radical elements in the North
that had criticised his delay now rallied to his support.

74. The Negro in the Civil War.—Negroes were
used by the Confederates long before they were used
by the Union forces. Even before the war actually
began they were employed in making redoubts and in
other rough work. Before the war was over, plans
for the formation of Negro regiments in the Confederate armies were seriously proposed, and General
Robert E. Lee was one of the strongest advocates of
such a policy. All such effort was of course at variance
with the main influences of the period, and the Negro
is naturally remembered most quickly in connection
with the Union armies. In May, 1861, while in command at Fortress Monroe, Major-General Benjamin
F. Butler came into prominence by receiving fugitive
slaves within his lines. He put these men to work

and justified their retention on the ground that, being
of service to the enemy for purposes of war, they were
like guns, powder, etc., "contraband of war," and
could not be reclaimed, On August 30th of this same
year Major-General John C. Fremont, in command
in Missouri, placed the state under martial law and
declared the slaves there emancipated. The administration was embarrassed, Fremont's order was annulled, and he was relieved of his command. On
May 9, 1862, Major-General David Hunter, in charge
of the Department of the South (that is, South Carolina, Georgia, and Florida) issued his famous order
freeing the slaves in his department, and thus brought
to general attention the matter of the employment of
Negro soldiers in the Union armies. The Confederate
government outlawed Hunter, Lincoln annulled his
order, and the grace of the nation was again saved; but
in the meantime a new situation had arisen. While
Brigadier-General John W. Phelps was taking part in
the expedition against New Orleans, a large sugar-
planter near the city, disgusted with federal interference with affairs on his plantation, drove all the
slaves away, telling them to go to their friends, the
Yankees. The Negroes came to Phelps in great numbers, and he attempted to organize them into troops.
Accordingly he too was outlawed by the Confederates,
and his act was disavowed by the Union, that was not

ready to take this step. It was not until a great many men had been killed, and until the Emancipation Proclamation had changed the status of the Negro, that steps were really taken by the Union for his employment as a soldier. Opinion in his favor gained force after the Draft Riot in New York, when Negroes in the city were persecuted by the enemies of conscription. Soon a distinct bureau was established in Washington for the recording of all matters pertaining to Negro troops, a board was organized for the examination of candidates, and recruiting stations were set up in Maryland, Missouri, and Tennessee. By the end of 1864 nearly 200,000 Negroes had been enrolled in the army. The Confederates were furious when they had to meet black men on equal footing, and refused to exchange Negro soldiers for white men. How such action was met by Stanton, Secretary of War, may be seen from the fact that when he learned that three Negro prisoners had been placed in close confinement, he ordered three South Carolina men to be treated likewise, the Confederate leaders being informed of his action. Such was the general progress of the Negro in the armies of the United States. Those Negroes who individually rose to distinction in the war, and the valor of the troops generally at Fort Wagner, Petersburg, and elsewhere, will receive more detailed consideration in our chapter on "The Negro as a Soldier."

75. Shaw and Higginson.—Of the commanders of Negro troops there were two who call for special notice. In January, 1863, Robert Gould Shaw, a young Harvard man in the Union army, was offered the colonelcy of the 54th Massachusetts, the first regiment of Negro troops raised in a Northern state. Although he knew that he would subject himself to severe criticism, he accepted. After taking part in an expedition to Florida, he was attacked by the forces operating against Fort Wagner, near Charleston, S. C., and on July 18, 1863, he was killed upon the parapet of the fort while leading an assault. Thus died at the age of twenty-six a young man who represented the fine flower of New England culture, and who should ever be honored for his noble faith and heroism. Edmonia Lewis, a sculptor of whose work we shall have more to say, attracted attention by a bust she made of him; and Saint-Gaudens designed a monument which now stands at the head of Boston Common just in front of the Massachusetts State House. The other distinguished commander of Negro troops was Thomas Wentworth Higginson. Already captain of a Massachusetts regiment of volunteers, this man became colonel of the first regiment of freed slaves raised in the United States. The ranks of this regiment included many men who had been slaves on Pierce Butler's plantation on St. Simon's Island, Georgia. By a wound received in a campaign in Florida in 1863 Colonel Higginson was forced to retire from the service; and after the war and until his death he devoted himself to literature and public affairs.

CHAPTER VIII

76. Difficulties of the Problem.—On arriving at the era of Reconstruction, we come to that period which is still the most hotly debated in American history. The enormous difficulties of the problem are hardly yet fully appreciated. The Civil War meant more than the emancipation of four million slaves, with all the perplexing questions that that liberation brought with it; it involved the overturning of the whole economic system of the South. A stroke of the pen had declared the bondmen free; but to educate these people, to train them in citizenship, and to give them a place in the new labor system, was all a problem for the wisest statesmanship and the largest and most intelligent patriotism. The Southern man, whose fortune was swept away, whose slaves were free, and whose father, son, or brother had died in battle, not unnaturally looked upon any legislation by the North as adding to his cup of humiliation. The North on the other hand was quick to interpret any effort by the white South in the readjustment of social and labor conditions as evidence of a refusal to accept in good

faith the results of the war. To increase the complica-
tion and the delicacy of the situation there were sometimes present personal or other peculiar elements
which seemed to contradict all the leading tendencies
of the period. Some Negroes, for instance, personally
attached to their masters, were unwilling to accept
their freedom; and generally throughout the South the
white people, who laid most of their ills at the door of
the Negro, resisted violently any considerable effort
toward migration on the part of the former slaves.
Such were but some of the things which increased the
difficulties of the problem in this era of shifting status.

77. Reconstruction. The War Amendments.—
According to the view of their status maintained by
the Southern states at the close of the war, each state
was theoretically indestructible, and the only thing
necessary for one to resume its former place in federal
councils was for it, having laid down its arms, to repeal
all acts that had looked toward disunion. According
to the view of President Lincoln, the act of rebellion
had been one not of the states themselves, but of certain disloyal persons who had subverted the government. Each *state* then continued to exist, and the
problem presented was simply to place the loyal elements in control. As this involved the use of the
pardoning power, the President regarded the matter
as one for executive rather than legislative authority.

Opposed to this was the opinion of Congress embodied in the Wade-Davis act of 1864, differing from the President's view in regarding the problem primarily as a legislative one, in requiring the loyalty of a majority of the white voters of a state as the basis of a reconstructed government instead of that of the one-tenth of the qualified voters of 1860 advocated by Lincoln, and in exacting for the Negro the full reality of his freedom and making sure the complete ascendancy of the victorious republican party over the Southern and Northern democrats who for so many years before the war had controlled national affairs. The leaders of this school of opinion were Charles Sumner, of Massachusetts, in the Senate, and Thaddeus Stevens, of Pennsylvania, in the House. The breach which opened between the President and Congress because of these conflicting views, but which Lincoln might have closed by his tact, fell to the lot of President Johnson, who, on May 29, 1865, issued a proclamation of amnesty with the understanding attached that those excluded from its benefits might make special application to him, and who, within the next few months, while Congress was not in session, worked out generally his theory of reconstruction. In the summer of 1865 conventions were held in the various Southern states, and in December the President informed Congress that with the exception of

Texas, whose convention did not meet until the following March, all the states had been reconstructed
and were ready to resume their places in Congress.
Because, however, of certain legislation in Mississippi, South Carolina, and Louisiana, embodied in
what were known as Black Codes, Congress doubted
whether the states were acting in good faith. These
Black Codes were in the nature of police regulations
ostensibly designed to prevent disorder and pauperism
among the freedmen, but were of such a nature
as to lead to the thought that they were really designed to curtail generally for the Negroes the benefits
of emancipation; and there was probability that other
states would go quite as far as those mentioned in the
passing of such acts. In the meantime the Thirteenth
Amendment to the Constitution had been sufficiently
ratified and was passed (Dec. 18, 1865), reading as
follows: "Neither slavery nor involuntary servitude,
except as a punishment for crime whereof the party
shall have been duly convicted, shall exist within the
United States, or any place subject to their jurisdiction. Congress shall have power to enforce this
article by appropriate legislation." Furthermore, in
March, 1866, Congress passed over the President's
veto the first Civil Rights Bill, guaranteeing to the
freedmen all the ordinary rights of citizenship; and it
enlarged the powers of the Freedmen's Bureau, which

had been recently established. At this point feeling in the North was intensified by some violent attacks on Negroes and white radicals in the South, especially by one such affair in New Orleans in which about forty men were killed and one hundred and fifty wounded. When Congress met in December, 1866, failing to impeach President Johnson, by various measures it limited his power, and then established Negro suffrage in the District of Columbia and the territories, and, urged on by the action of the Southern states in rejecting the proposed Fourteenth Amendment, it proceeded to divide the ten states which had seceded into five military districts, as follows: (1) Virginia, (2) North and South Carolina, (3) Georgia, Florida, and Alabama, (4) Mississippi and Arkansas, (5) Louisiana and Texas. Military law now protected everybody in the enjoyment of the rights of person and property, and oversaw the registration and voting of all men without regard to race or color. By February, 1868, conventions were in session in every state that had seceded. These were made up very largely of the freedmen, of Northern men who had come South since the war and who were called in derision "carpetbaggers," and Southern men who acted at variance with the prevailing sentiment of the South and who were known as "scalawags." Moreover, secret organizations, of which the Union League was the best example, were formed for marshalling the Negro vote for the republican party. The Fourteenth Amendment, as finally passed by Congress (July 28, 1868), denied to the states the power to abridge the privileges or immunities of citizens of the United States, or to deprive any person of life, liberty, or property without due process of law; and enacted that if a state discriminated against any class of citizens in voting privileges, its representation in the national Congress was to be decreased proportionately. The third section of the amendment excluded from all national and state offices (except under a two-thirds vote of Congress) all persons "who, having previously taken an oath . . . to support the Constitution of the United States, shall have engaged in insurrection or rebellion against the same, or even given aid or comfort to the enemies thereof." At the time when Grant came to the presidency (1869), four states (Virginia, Mississippi, Texas, and Georgia) had still not accepted the new settlement. By July 15, 1870, however, when Georgia was admitted, they had all been forced to accept the Fifteenth Amendment (passed March 30, 1870), which sought to protect the Negro in the right of suffrage instead of giving to him a guarantee of military protection. This amendment read: "The right of citizens of the United States to vote shall not be denied or abridged by the United States or by any state, on account of race, color, or previous condition of servitude. The Congress shall have power to enforce this article by appropriate legislation." The carpetbag governments were now in full career, and there set in an era of extravagance, plunder, and increasing debt in which for the most part the carpetbaggers and the scalawags rather than the Negroes reaped the benefit. Then it was that the KuKlux Klan began to terrorize Negroes with a view to preventing them from exercising their political rights. In 1875 was passed the second Civil Rights Act, which was designed to give Negroes equality of treatment in theaters, railway cars, hotels, etc.; but this the Supreme Court declared unconstitutional in 1883. Meanwhile the withdrawal of the federal troops and the wholesale removal of disabilities by Congress weakened the reconstruction governments and made possible democratic success in the South.

78. Freedmen's Bureau.—Such is a bare outline of political events in the South in the chaotic era succeeding the war. Some subjects prompted by this review, however, are deserving of more than passing attention. One of these is the Freedmen's Bureau. This was not exactly a missionary organization, but its efforts were largely philanthropic, and it became connected with more distinctively missionary enterprises. It was created as a charge of the War Department by an act of March 3, 1865, and was to remain in existence throughout the war and for one year thereafter. Its powers were enlarged, however, by an act of July 16, 1866. "It was rendered necessary by the presence within the Federal lines of vast numbers of Negroes who had escaped or had been rescued from slavery, and of whom at least a million were at the time of the passing of the act dependent for support upon the Federal Government." * The Freedmen's Bureau was to have the "supervision and management of all abandoned lands, and the control of all subjects relating to refugees and freedmen." Of special importance was the provision that authorized the President to appropriate for the use of freedmen the confiscated and abandoned lands within the Southern states; each male refugee was to be given forty acres with the guarantee of possession for three years. The Bureau's chief work ended January 1, 1869; its educational work was continued for a year and a half longer. When it came to an end, it turned its educational interests and much money over to the religious and benevolent societies which had co-operated with it, especially to the American Missionary Association. Throughout the existence of the Freedmen's Bureau its chief commissioner was Gen. O. O. Howard. While its principal officers were un-

* *Nelson's Encyclopedia*, Article *Freedmen's Bureau.*

doubtedly men of noble purpose, many of the minor officials were just as undoubtedly corrupt and self-seeking. Altogether it established 4,239 schools in the South for Negro pupils, and these had 9,307 teachers and 247,333 students.* Its real achievement has been thus ably summed up: "The greatest success of the Freedmen's Bureau lay in the planting of the free school among Negroes, and the idea of free elementary education among all classes in the South. . . . For some fifteen million dollars, beside the sum spent before 1865, and the dole of benevolent societies, this bureau set going a system of free labor, established a beginning of peasant proprietorship, secured the recognition of black freedmen before courts of law, and founded the free common school in the South. On the other hand, it failed to begin the establishment of good will between ex-masters and freedmen, to guard its work wholly from paternalistic methods which discouraged self-reliance, and to carry out to any considerable extent its implied promises to furnish the freedmen with land." † To this tale of its shortcomings must be added also the management of the Freedmen's Bank, which "was morally and practically part of the Freedmen's Bureau, although it had no legal connection with it." This institution made a

* Andrew Carnegie, *The Negro in America*, 23.
† DuBois, *The Souls of Black Folk*, 32–37.

really remarkable start in the development of thrift among the Negroes, and its failure, involving the loss of the first savings of hundreds of ex-slaves, was as disastrous in its moral as in its immediate financial consequences.

79. Representative Negroes.—Deserving at least of passing notice in this interesting period is the large number of Negroes that the new order of events brought into prominence. The freedmen were not only very active in Southern legislatures, but were also frequently sent to Congress. Mississippi sent Hiram R. Revels and Blanche K. Bruce to the United States Senate, and a considerable number of Negroes went to the House of Representatives. South Carolina was represented by Robert C. DeLarge, Alonzo J. Ransier, Joseph H. Rainey, Robert Smalls, and Robert B. Elliott; Alabama sent James T. Rapier, and Mississippi John R. Lynch. Oscar J. Dunn, P. B. S. Pinchback, and C. C. Antoine became lieutenant-governors of Louisiana; Richard H. Gleaves and Alonzo J. Ransier held the same position in South Carolina, and Alexander Davis in Mississippi. Of all these men the foremost for general ability were Robert B. Elliott and Blanche K. Bruce. Elliott was born in Boston, received a good education in England, and, returning to America, developed highly the arts of a politician. In Congress he attracted attention by a speech in reply to Alexander Stephens of Georgia on the constitutionality of the Civil Rights Bill. Bruce was well informed on matters pertaining to the race, and in the course of his life held several public offices besides the senatorship. For two separate terms (1881-5 and 1897-8) he was Register of the Treasury.

80. KuKlux Klan.—An important consideration in this era of change is the means by which the white people of the South regained political power. Even before the war a secret organization, the Knights of the Golden Circle, had been formed to advance Southern interests; but far more important than anything of this nature that had preceded it was the KuKlux Klan.* This organization began in Tennessee in 1866 as an association of young men for amusement, and its membership included some of the representative citizens of the Old South. It soon developed, however, into a union for the purpose of whipping, banishing, terrorizing, and murdering Negroes and Northern white men who encouraged them in the exercise of their political rights. The costume of the members especially was designed to play upon the superstitious nature of the uneducated Negroes. "Loose flowing sleeves [were worn], with a hood, in which the apertures for the eyes, nose and mouth were trimmed with some **red** material. The hood had also three horns, made

* From Greek κύκλος meaning *circle*, and the English *clan*.

of some common cotton-stuff, standing out on its front and sides."* The KuKlux Klan finally extended over the whole South, being highly developed in its organization; and it greatly increased its operations on the cessation of martial law in 1870. As it worked generally at night with its members in disguise, it was difficult for a grand jury to get evidence on which to frame a bill, and almost impossible to get a jury that would return a verdict for the state. Repeated measures against the order were of little effect until an act of 1870 extended the jurisdiction of the United States courts to all KuKlux cases. After this the Klan declined and eventually died out.

81. Negro Exodus.—The aftermath of the whole reconstruction era was what was known as the Negro Exodus. By 1879 conditions in the South had changed so much that Negroes were denied political recognition, were charged exorbitant prices by many merchants, were forced to pay excessive rents, and generally kept down in every possible way. At last in some localities, especially in Mississippi, Louisiana, and Texas, the state of affairs became so bad as to be no longer tolerable. A general convention of Negroes held in Nashville in May, 1879, adopted a report that set forth their grievances and encouraged emigration to the North and West, where rights would not

* Fleming, II, 364.

be denied. Thousands now left their homes in the South, going in greatest numbers to Kansas, Missouri, and Indiana. Within about twenty months Kansas alone thus received an addition to her population of 40,000 Negroes. Many of these people arrived at their destination practically penniless and with no prospect of immediate employment. Large sums of money for their relief were raised throughout the North, however, and gradually they found a place in their new homes. In the Southeast there was also some movement in the same direction. One account says that in one note-worthy week about 5,000 Negroes removed from South Carolina to Arkansas. This part of the country was also remarkable for an effort in another direction. In 1877 the Liberian Exodus Joint Stock Company was formed by the Negroes with the threefold purpose of sending emigrants to Africa, of bringing African products to America, and of establishing a regular steamship line between Monrovia and Charleston. In this enterprise Baptists and Methodists joined hands, and at an expense of $7,000 a vessel, the *Azor*, was purchased in Boston. The white people of Charleston, who not only did not wish to lose their labor but who also realized the possibilities of the company as a business enterprise, sought to embar-rass the promoters in every possible way. Although the *Azor* had recently been repaired in Boston, they induced the custom house officials not to grant it clearance papers until a new copper bottom had been put on it at an expense of $2,000. Moreover, not all the people the vessel could hold were allowed to go on the first trip. Finally, through the treachery of the captain and his connivance with prominent business men of Charleston, the *Azor* was stolen and sold in Liverpool. One gets an interesting sidelight on conditions in these times when he knows that even the United States Circuit Court in South Carolina refused to entertain the suit brought by the Negroes.

CHAPTER IX

82. The Pioneers.—Dr. DuBois has pointed out four periods in Negro education since the Civil War: (1) From 1865 to 1876, the period of uncertain groping and temporary relief, with army schools, mission schools, and schools of the Freedmen's Bureau in chaotic disarrangement; (2) Then a decade of definite effort toward the building of complete school systems, with normal schools and colleges training teachers for the public schools; (3) From 1885 to 1895, the springing into notice of the industrial school; and (4) Since 1895 the full recognition of the industrial school as the answer to a combined educational and economic crisis. Too much credit can hardly be given to the heroic men and women who labored in the first of these periods. Those people of the North who took upon themselves the education of the Negro immediately after the war had no enviable task. They had as their lot only prejudice and ostracism, and an infinite amount of hard work; and their only reward was a high sense of duty well done. Where so many were noble it is almost unjust to mention names; but in any case deserving of honor were General Armstrong at Hampton, President Cravath at Fisk, President Tupper at Shaw, President Ware at Atlanta University, and, of a slightly later date, at Spelman Seminary, Presidents Sophia B. Packard and Harriet E. Giles. Just as earnest as such teachers as these were those who devoted themselves to mission work in the homes of the freedmen, of whom a sterling example was Joanna P. Moore, who for fifty years labored in the cause of her Fireside Schools.

83. Philanthropy.—For the execution of the task at hand money was needed, and private philanthropy was not lacking, though even the most princely gifts were inadequate for the great work to be done. In 1867 George Peabody, a great American merchant and patriot, established the Peabody Educational Fund for the purpose of promoting "intellectual, moral, and industrial education in the most destitute portion of the Southern states." In all cases the trustees of this fund worked in unison with state and local authorities. In the first thirty years of its existence a total of more than $2,500,000 was distributed in the South, Dr. J. L. M. Curry being one of the agents. In 1888 Daniel Hand of Connecticut gave $1,000,000 to the American Missionary Association. In 1882 John F. Slater established an endowment for the encouragement of industrial education among

the Negroes in the South. The annual income from this has been about $60,000, and Bishop Atticus G. Haygood and Dr. Curry were for certain periods agents of the fund. In recent years the Peabody and Slater boards have become closely affiliated with the General Education Board and the Southern Education Board of New York, the General Education Board being the medium of the philanthropy of John D. Rockefeller.

84. Howard University.—In addition to such private giving as this, it is to be noted that the United States Government in 1867 crowned its work for the education of the Negro by the establishment at Washington of Howard University. This institution, named for General O. O. Howard, has stood for the highest collegiate and professional training of the Negro; and its Teachers College and its Medical School are widely distinguished for their peculiar emphasis. To the resources of its own laboratories and library it adds the advantages of an institution located at the national capital and fostered by the government. In all departments there were in 1917–18, 1,565 students, the College of Arts and Sciences and the Teachers College together enrolling 519 students, a much larger number of students of collegiate grade than is to be found in any other institution emphasizing the education of the Negro. In the far South the chief efforts for education were those put forth by the various missionary organizations of the North.

85. American Missionary Association.—One of the unfortunate but practically inevitable characteristics of missionary endeavor in Negro education was the utter independence of one another of all the efforts put forth by the different religious organizations. The American Missionary Association was organized before the Civil War on an interdenominational and strong anti-slavery basis. With the withdrawal of general interest, however, this body passed in 1881 into the hands of the Congregational Church. It was the first of all the benevolent organizations to begin educational work, opening a school in Hampton, Va., in 1861, and founding immediately after the war its permanent institutions. It was decided to establish one school of higher learning in each of the larger states of the South, normal and graded schools in the principal cities, and common and parochial schools in smaller villages and country places. Under this plan arose Hampton in Virginia, Atlanta University in Georgia, Berea College in Kentucky, Fisk University in Tennessee, Straight University in Louisiana, Talladega College in Alabama, Tougaloo University in Mississippi, and Tillotson College in Texas. Hampton and Atlanta University are now independent; and Berea has had a peculiar history, legislation having compelled the withdrawal of her Negro students a few years ago. Fisk is noted for her comparatively large number of college graduates and for her emphasis on music. One of the most inspiring chapters in her history is that of the Jubilee Singers, of whose interesting career we shall have more to say in our chapter on "Literature and Art." Atlanta University has in recent years attracted national attention by her original studies of questions relating to the Negro, these being conducted under the auspices of the Atlanta Conference. Theological departments have been established at Fisk, Talladega, and Straight; and generally the American Missionary Association has emphasized manual and industrial as well as collegiate training, Talladega College having antedated all other schools in establishing an industrial department. Besides its institutions of collegiate grade, the Association now maintains more than forty normal and graded schools, and more than thirty common schools. The normal and graded schools include the Avery Institute in Charleston, the Le-Moyne in Memphis, the Beach in Savannah, the Ballard Normal in Macon, Ga., and the Lincoln Normal in Marion, Ark. Generally representative of the secondary schools is the Joseph K. Brick Agricultural, Industrial and Normal School in Enfield, N. C., which has 10 buildings and 1,129 acres of land.

86. American Baptist Home Mission Society.— The first step by the American Baptist Home Mission Society for the refugees who came into the lines of the Union army was taken in January, 1862; and the first teachers were appointed in June of this year. From the first the idea of religious education was prominent in the efforts in behalf of the freedmen. Wherever they could do so, the teachers brought together the Negro preachers for instruction in the rudiments of learning and for the organization of churches, associations, and conventions. This ideal of an educated ministry becomes important when one remembers how great an influence preachers have among the Negro people, and how many of the people are Baptists. Gradually, to meet the demand for the education of the young people, institutions of learning were established, and the work of the Society has expanded until it now embraces a chain of schools. This organization has moreover helped a great many schools which are owned by Negroes. The schools of higher learning that the Society now owns and operates (in some cases in cooperation with the Women's American Baptist Home Mission Society) are eight in number, as follows: two devoted to the education of young men, Morehouse College and Virginia Union University; two devoted to the training of young women, Spelman Seminary in Atlanta and Hartshorn Memorial College in

Richmond; four that are co-educational, Bishop College in Marshall, Texas, Benedict College in Columbia, S. C., Shaw University in Raleigh, N. C., and Jackson College in Jackson, Miss. These schools are supposed to be of the same rank; but as a matter of fact, with the exception of the co-operation of Morehouse College and Spelman Seminary, they are not co-ordinated, and as they have developed they have consciously or unconsciously emphasized very different things. Perhaps a little more than the others Morehouse College and Virginia Union University have laid stress on regular college work. Prominent in theological training is Virginia Union, whose department was formerly the Richmond Theological Seminary. Several others of the institutions, however, also offer divinity training. Spelman Seminary is the largest institution in the world devoted solely to the education of Negro young women. It enrolled in all departments in 1917–18 817 students. The collegiate work is in connection with that of Morehouse College; but the school is best known for its training of teachers and nurses, for its emphasis on domestic science, and for its constant ideal of Christian womanhood. Spelman has moreover in the record of her graduates who have gone as missionaries to Africa a tradition as glorious as that of the Fisk Jubilee Singers. Benedict has for some years had a good band. Shaw in former years, even more than now, placed 'emphasis on professional training. In connection with the American Baptist Home Mission Society mention should also be made of the American Baptist Publication Society, an organization which after the Civil War by institutes and Bible distribution did a great deal for the education of Negro Baptist ministers, but whose activities have in recent years been greatly curtailed by the success of the distinctively Negro enterprise, the National Baptist Publishing Board.

87. Freedmen's Aid Society.—As will be seen later, a consideration of the educational work of most of the Methodist denominations belongs to the chapter on Self-Help in Negro Education rather than to that on Missionary Endeavor. The Freedmen's Aid and Southern Education Society, however, was organized by the Northern Methodists in 1866 and was purely missionary in its purpose. From the first it has been prominent in the work in the South. It now supports twenty-four institutions. Several of these are collegiate in scope, among them being Clark University in South Atlanta, Ga., Claflin University in Orangeburg, S. C., New Orleans University in New Orleans, La., Rust University in Holly Springs, Miss., Wiley University in Marshall, Texas, Bennett College in Greensboro, N. C., the

George R. Smith College in Sedalia, Mo., Morgan College in Baltimore, Md., and Philander Smith College in Little Rock, Ark. In connection with Walden is the Meharry Medical School. Gammon Theological Seminary in South Atlanta, Ga., is the most thoroughly equipped and the best endowed theological seminary in the entire South, and as an institution for the education of Negro ministers it is the most thoroughly equipped and the best endowed in the world.

88. **Presbyterian Board of Missions.**—In 1882, after the missionary work of various Presbyterian committees had for some time been consolidated, the resulting central committee became incorporated as "The Board of Missions for Freedmen of the Presbyterian Church in the United States of America." This organization has been active in church as well as school work; but its purely religious activities must be reserved for consideration in connection with the Negro Church. Even before the War, in 1854, a Presbyterian minister, John M. Dickey, established in Pennsylvania Ashmun Institute, later and better known as Lincoln University. The larger part of the work of the Presbyterian Board lies in North Carolina, South Carolina, and southern Virginia. With Lincoln University the most prominent institutions are Biddle University, in Charlotte, N. C., and the five seminaries for girls, Ingleside in Burkeville, Va., Scotia in Con-

cord, N. C., Barber Memorial in Anniston, Ala., Mary
Holmes in West Point, Miss., and Mary Allen in
Crockett, Texas. To these institutions must be added
over seventy academies and parochial schools. Besides the work of the Presbyterian Board of Missions considerable work is done by the United and
the Southern Presbyterians, the United Presbyterians maintaining Knoxville College in Knoxville,
Tenn.

89. Other Agencies.—The four large organizations
just considered have been responsible for most of the
work done in the South for the high school and collegiate training of the Negro. This of course takes
no account of the state schools; and those which the
Negro has built for himself are yet to be considered.
The state schools have in recent years greatly emphasized agricultural training, with a corresponding
lowering of literary standards. The one in Talla-
hassee, Fla., however, is above the average in technical
studies. A full study of missionary enterprises would
also consider the work of the Episcopalians and the
Catholics. Prominent Episcopal schools are the St.
Paul Normal and Industrial School at Lawrenceville,
Va., and St. Augustine's School in Raleigh, N. C.
Roman Catholics operate St. Joseph's Industrial
School for Colored Boys in Clayton, Del., St. Augustine's Academy in Lebanon, Ky., and St. Frances'

Academy in Baltimore. Altogether they had at last accounts in the United States for Negro children about one hundred schools with an attendance of 10,000; but they have made remarkable advance within the last few years, especially in the South.

90. Scholarship in the Schools.—Whatever may be the name of an institution mentioned in this chapter, no one is as yet a fully equipped university, as no one yet maintains a graduate school. Howard, however, with its professional departments and with its peculiar environment and support, has already made some beginning in graduate study, and needs only a little more emphasis in this direction to satisfy every possible standard. Because of the inadequate training given in the common schools of the South, only Howard has so far found it advisable to cut off all literary departments below the college. Even those that are foremost still retain their academies. The best basis for a study of the scholarship in these institutions is the standing that their graduates attain and maintain in the great Northern universities. Judged by this standard the graduates of some of the poorer of the colleges are in real ability not equal to the boy who has just graduated from St. Paul's or from Worcester Academy. There are, however, ten or twelve institutions in which a very different standard is maintained, and graduates from these are sometimes required to spend only a year at a Northern university before receiving the degree of Bachelor of Arts, if indeed they do not choose to enter a graduate school at once. In every case much depends on the individual. As a matter of fact the Southern Negro graduate most often maintains very high standing in the North— naturally, for he is frequently the picked man from his college. One of the most interesting things about this continuation of study is the preference shown by certain schools in the South for certain ones in the North. This is generally determined by the success at the great Northern university of one or two of the earlier graduates of the Negro college; thus, while exceptions may of course be found, Atlanta University men go to Harvard, Morehouse College men to the University of Chicago, and Talladega men most frequently go to Yale. All of this of course takes no account of those Negro students who pursue their whole course in a Northern college. Those who have thus studied and graduated now number about eight hundred. The whole matter of the efficiency of the work of a Negro college depends on the ability of the students who are admitted to it. The college preparatory course then becomes of supreme importance; and it is here where standards ought to be highest that the greatest divergency appears. The three or four institutions of the highest rank, however, insist on all the standards of the Carnegie Foundation, and sometimes exact even more than these demand.

91. Collegiate Activities.—Life in these schools seeks an outlet in various channels. Within the last ten years the college idea has been much developed. Among other activities intercollegiate debating has received considerable attention. Early in 1910 Howard, Fisk, and Atlanta University formed a triangular debating league, and in 1911 Morehouse, Knoxville, and Talladega did the same, though Morehouse and Talladega, beginning their contests in 1906, have maintained longer unbroken relations than any other institutions. Several schools, notably Hampton, Shaw, Fisk, and Atlanta University have from time to time sent quartettes through the North to raise money by singing the old melodies. The Fisk singers have perhaps been most noteworthy, and the annual concert of the Mozart Society of this institution is always an important event in Nashville. Several of the schools present each year an entire English play, and all of them cultivate athletics, although only here and there are real gymnasium facilities to be found. In Y. M. C. A. work Morehouse College seems to have been especially prominent. In the fall of 1918 practically all of the larger or more prominent institutions were selected for the formation of units of the Students' Army Training Corps, Howard University in the summer of this year having been designated as the place of training for student or acting non-commissioned officers.

92. Outlook for the Colleges.—The outlook for these institutions is not so bright as it should be. Those that are independent have had to weather some stormy seasons. With the possible exception of Gammon Theological Seminary, no one is adequately endowed, though here and there, as at Benedict, Fisk, Spelman, and Atlanta University, some beginning in this direction has been made. The dominance in recent years of the idea of industrial education for Negroes has directed the means of philanthropists most largely toward schools which emphasize this kind of training. There is, however, no real conflict between the industrial school and the college. Each has an important function to fulfill, and each deserves support. Very frequently the colleges have been criticised as placing too much emphasis on philosophical and theoretical subjects and on the classics. This was due to some extent to the traditions under which their founders labored, and in some measure also to their general lack of means for adequate teaching and laboratory facilities. In various ways, however, constructive efforts are being made to bring them into more vital touch with the communities that they are supposed to serve. Especially is there a demand also for more economy and co-operation in effort. The colleges themselves have made an excellent beginning toward meeting this. In 1913 eight of the representative institutions—Howard University, Wilberforce University, Knoxville College, Fisk University, Virginia Union University, Atlanta University, Morehouse College, and Talladega College—organized the Association of Colleges for Negro Youth, the general purposes of this association being insistence on standard college entrance requirements, and mutual helpfulness in all the problems incident to the work of colleges so closely related in their work. Shaw, Benedict, and Bishop have also been taken into the organization, and it is destined to have wider and wider influence on higher education in the South.

93. Results of the Work.—Most of the graduates of these institutions are of course those from high school courses. Negro college graduates in the United States now number altogether about seven thousand. The figure would have to be increased fivefold in order to sustain to the total Negro population the same ratio as that held by the total number of college graduates in the country to the total population. Recent statistics show that fifty-four per cent of these graduates are engaged in teaching and twenty per cent in preaching. In conclusion we may accept with reference to the results of the work the word of two men who had exceptional opportunities for study of the subject and who may be said to speak generally for the experience of the Northern organizations. Said Dr. H. L. Morehouse of the American Baptist Home Mission Society : " In my years of service for the Society I have seen the coarse country boy become the talented preacher, the cultured professor, and the wise leader of thousands, and from long and wide acquaintance and observation I am prepared to say that the investment has paid a hundredfold; " and Dr. James W. Cooper of the American Missionary Association said : " The people have advanced. Their progress has been phenomenal. The record of forty years is one of inspiration and encouragement as we look back upon the brave and patient struggles of this lowly people, out of the disabilities of slavery into the good estate of a self-respecting freedom."

CHAPTER X

94. Negro Suffrage before the Civil War.—At the time of the making of the Constitution, free Negroes could become voters in every one of the thirteen states except South Carolina and Georgia. Delaware, by an act of 1792, was the first one of the other states to discriminate against Negroes in the suffrage. The other middle states gradually followed her example, and even Connecticut in 1814 did likewise. Disqualification had advanced so far at the time of the Civil War that "things had come to the point where Negroes could vote only in five New England states, and (under special restrictions) in New York." *

95. The Sequel of Reconstruction.—We have seen how the results of the Civil War were summed up in the Thirteenth Amendment, which abolished slavery, in the Fourteenth, which conferred citizenship on the former slaves, and in the Fifteenth, which protected them in the right to vote. Whatever may have been the faults of the reconstruction era, such was the

* Hart.

lack of opportunity for education that the freedmen had possessed, and such was the complexity of issues raised in the period, that " the speedy breaking up of Negro suffrage practically left little time for any complete proof as to the capacity or discretion of the Negro." Nevertheless the South decided very soon not to try the experiment again if it could keep from doing so. In the decade 1870–80 intimidation; theft, suppression, or exchange of the ballot boxes; removal of the polls to unknown places; false certifications; and illegal arrests on the day before an election were the chief means used by the South to make the Negro vote of little effect. Soon the Republican party in the South declined, and after a while the Democrats refused to admit Negroes to their primaries. Generally after 1871 the Negro vote was in one way or another rendered ineffectual in every state in the South.

96. Changing Opinion.—Such a situation is to be accounted for not only by the shortcomings of the Negro, for it is indeed coming more and more to be recognized that these have been exaggerated, and it is now well known that he did much for the promotion of such good work as that of common school education; the changes in the new era rather find their explanation in the larger forces at work in the general life of the American people. Again might one speak of the

"decline of great convictions." After the spiritual elevation of the Civil War, the country, about 1870, descended into a period of industrialism, of opportunism, and even of scandal and dishonesty in high places. It was an age of materialism, not one of high moral principle; and in the stress of commercialism the Negro ceased to be an issue. As for him, indeed, the era was formally signalized by one of the most effective speeches ever delivered in this or any other country, all the more forceful because the orator was a man of unusual nobility of spirit. In 1886 Henry W. Grady, of Georgia, addressed the New England Club in New York on "The New South." He spoke to practical men and he knew his ground. He asked his hearers to bring their "full faith in American fairness and frankness" to judgment upon what he had to say. He pictured in brilliant language the Confederate soldier, "ragged, half-starved, heavy-hearted, who wended his way homeward to find his house in ruins and his farm devastated." He also spoke kindly of the Negro: "Whenever he struck a blow for his own liberty he fought in open battle, and when at last he raised his black and humble hands that the shackles might be struck off, those hands were innocent of wrong against his helpless charges." But Grady also implied that the Negro had received too much attention and sympathy from the North. Said he: " To liberty and enfranchisement is as far as law can carry the Negro. The rest must be left to conscience and common sense." Hence he asked that the South be left alone in the handling of her grave problem. The North, largely assenting to this request, became more indifferent about the whole question of the Negro, and very fast there developed evils which Henry W. Grady, with his large humanity, could certainly never have countenanced.

97. Peonage and Other Evils.—One of the first of these evils to force attention was the peonage that was most frequently an outgrowth of the convict lease system. A noteworthy feature of legislation enacted in the South immediately after the Civil War was severe provision with reference to vagrancy. Negroes were often arrested on the slightest pretexts and their labor as that of convicts leased to landowners or other business men. When moreover Negroes, dissatisfied with their returns under the developing " share " system of labor, began a movement to the cities where better industrial opportunities were offered, there arose a tendency to make the vagrancy legislation still more harsh, so that more and more a laborer could not stop work without technically committing a crime. The abuses of the convict lease system at length arrested general attention, but meanwhile other evils had developed apace. In the period

1871–73 the number of Negroes lynched in the South is said to have been not more than 11 a year. In the year 1892, however, there were 235 lynchings in the country, and in 1893 200, almost all of these being of Negroes in the South. Altogether within a period of thirty-five years 3,200 Negro men and women were lynched within the boundaries of the United States, an average of just a little less than 100 a year. Moreover, separate and inferior traveling accommodations, especially meager provision for the education of Negro children, inadequate street, lighting, and water facilities in most cities and towns, and the general lack of protection of life and property, especially in the rural districts, made life all the harder for the Negro people. Nevertheless they made rapid progress. By 1900 exactly 20 per cent of those in the Southern states were living in owned homes. In the decade ending with this year moreover they were still a considerable political factor in different communities of the South, as when in North Carolina a fusion of Republicans and Populists sent a Negro, George H. White, to Congress, thus defeating and alarming the Democrats. This incident, however, served only to strengthen the movement for disfranchisement which had already begun.

98. Progress of Disfranchisement.—However suppressed the Negro's vote may have been in actual practice, not until 1890 was he disfranchised in any state by direct legislation. In this year the Constitution of Mississippi was so amended as to exclude from the suffrage any person who had not paid his poll-tax or who was unable to read any section of the Constitution, or understand it when read to him, or to give a reasonable interpretation of it. The effect of the administration of this provision was the exclusion of the great majority of the Negroes. South Carolina amended her constitution with similar effect in 1895. In 1898 Louisiana passed an amendment inventing the so-called "grandfather clause." This excused from the operation of her disfranchising act all descendants of men who had voted before the Civil War, thus admitting to the suffrage all white men who were illiterate and without property. North Carolina in 1900, Virginia and Alabama in 1901, Georgia in 1907, and Oklahoma in 1910 in one way or another practically disfranchised the Negro, care being taken in every instance to avoid any flagrant violation of the Fifteenth Amendment. In Maryland there have been three distinct efforts to disfranchise the Negro by constitutional amendments, one in 1905, another in 1909, and the last in 1911, all failing by large majorities.

99. Summary of the Legislation.—However much they may have differed in detail, the disfranchising acts " had three points in common : (a) Some device enabling all the white voters to evade the force of the disfranchising clauses; (b) The limiting clauses themselves which deprive a majority of the colored voters of their franchise ; (c) The reservation of sufficient discretionary power in boards of registrars to enable them to give full effect to the acknowledged purpose of the framers of the [new or amended] constitutions." *   In six of the disfranchising states—Louisiana, North Carolina, Alabama, Virginia, Georgia, and Oklahoma—the suffrage limitations are more narrowly restricted by the " grandfather clause," which gives exemption from the restrictions to soldiers and their sons and grandsons (Louisiana);   to persons who had a right to vote prior to 1867 and to their lineal descendants (North Carolina);   to soldiers and their lawful descendants (Alabama) ; to soldiers and sailors who served in time of war prior to 1902 and to their sons (Virginia); to soldiers and their descendants (Georgia).   The word *soldier* has of course practical reference to those who fought in the Confederate army in the Civil War.   Only those who should register prior to December 31, 1898, in Louisiana; to December 1, 1908, in North Carolina ; to January 1, 1903, in Alabama ; to December 31, 1903, in Virginia ; and to the year 1911 in Georgia, and who had paid their poll-taxes regularly could claim the benefit of exemption.

* Charles C. Cook, in *The Negro and the Elective Franchise*, 20.

" Under the permanent registration provisions, educational qualifications are fixed for those without property, and property qualifications are prescribed in the case of illiterates. Thus the Alabama constitution admitted to the suffrage those owning at least forty acres of land, or real and personal property assessed at a valuation of at least $300." * The disfranchising amendment to the constitution of the state of Georgia is fairly typical of some of the more specific provisions of the disfranchising acts. In this state any male person of legal age who has paid his poll-tax may register and vote if he can read accurately or write accurately a paragraph of the state constitution that may be read to him. Any person owning or paying taxes on $500 worth of property may register and vote whether literate or illiterate. The provision that really eliminates the Negro is the one so common in the disfranchising amendments to the effect that the registrars may use their discretion in admitting any candidate for registration who is of good character and who understands the duties of citizenship.

100. Supreme Court Decision.—Naturally all such legislation as that just outlined had ultimately to be brought before the highest tribunal in the country. The test came over the following section from the Oklahoma law : " No person shall be registered as an

* *Nelson's Encyclopedia,* Article *Disfranchisement.*

elector of this state or be allowed to vote in any election herein unless he shall be able to read and write
any section of the Constitution of the State of Oklahoma; but no person who was on January 1, 1866, or
at any time prior thereto, entitled to vote under any
form of government, or who at any time resided in some
foreign nation, and no lineal descendant of such person
shall be denied the right to register and vote because
of his inability to so read and write sections of such
Constitution." This enactment the Supreme Court
declared unconstitutional in 1915. The decision
exerted no great and immediate effect on political
conditions in the South; nevertheless as the official
recognition by the nation of the fact that the Negro
was not accorded his full political rights, even though
this recognition was greatly delayed, it was destined
ultimately to have far-reaching effect on the whole
political fabric of the South.

101. The Negro as a Political Force.—When the
era of disfranchisement began it was of course in large
measure expected by the South that with the practical
elimination of the Negro from politics this section
would become wider in its outlook and divide on national issues. Such has not proved to be the case.
The South remains just as " solid " as it was thirty-
five years ago, largely of course because the Negro,
through education and the acquisition of property,

is becoming more and more a potential factor in politics. Meanwhile it is to be observed that the Negro is not wholly without the vote, even in the South. In the North moreover—especially in Indiana, Ohio, New Jersey, Illinois, Pennsylvania, and New York—he has power that on some occasions has even proved the deciding factor in political affairs. Even when not voting, however, he involuntarily wields tremendous influence on the destinies of the nation, for even though men may be disfranchised, all are nevertheless counted in the allotment of congressmen to Southern states. In the presidential election of 1912 Massachusetts sent 18 electors to the electoral college and South Carolina 9; but for her 18 Massachusetts cast 488,156 votes, and for her 9 South Carolina cast 50,348. In 1914 Kansas and Mississippi each elected eight members of the House of Representatives, but Kansas had to cast 483,683 votes for her members, while Mississippi cast only 37,185 for hers, less than one-twelfth as many. For the remedying of this situation by the enforcement of the Fourteenth Amendment to the effect that the basis of representation shall be reduced in the proportion that the voting of adult male citizens is reduced, bills have frequently been presented in Congress; but so far no definite action has been taken.

CHAPTER XI

102. Hampton Institute.—Hampton Normal and Agricultural Institute was opened in April, 1868, under the auspices of the American Missionary Association, with General Samuel Chapman Armstrong in charge. In 1870 it was chartered by a special act of the General Assembly of Virginia and thus became independent. The aim of the school was expressed by its founder in the following words: "To train selected youth who shall go out and teach and lead their people, first by example by getting land and homes; to give them not a dollar that they can earn for themselves; to teach respect for labor; to replace stupid drudgery with skilled hands; and to these ends to build up an industrial system, for the sake of character." On the Institute grounds there are 113 buildings, including instructors' cottages, and at Shellbanks, six miles distant, there are 22 buildings; 76 of the buildings were erected by student labor. The home farm contains 120 acres, and the one at Shellbanks about 600. Opportunity is afforded for a great diversity of farm

operations, and it is intended that every boy who
graduates from the academic department shall have
some skill in the building arts, and that every girl
shall be correspondingly expert in domestic science.
The course of study emphasizes English composition
and subjects of current interest. A summer school for
teachers is held, and an annual conference in July
brings together some of the best representatives of the
race, considering such subjects as The Relation of the
School to the Community; Country Life; Health;
the Sunday-School; Life Insurance; Co-operation as a
Means of Progress. In 1917-18 the enrollment, excluding the normal practice school, was 900; including
this school it was 1373. The practical nature of the
work at Hampton, the thoroughness of the training,
the military discipline, the opportunity for technical
education, and the beauty of the location have made
the school deservedly famous.

103. The Time and the Man.—Here then at Hampton Institute was developing a marvellous equipment,
emphasis being given to matters of daily interest and
concern. Hardly anyone realized in 1880 how much
the sort of training here given was in accord with the
industrial spirit so soon to make itself felt in the South.
For a decade young men and women had been sent
forth with the message of cleaner and thriftier living;
but their activity had been confined almost wholly to

Virginia. The thing needed was for some strong man to go down to the cotton belt, interpret the lesson for the men and women digging in the ground, teach them better methods, and generally place them in line with the South's development. The man was ready in the person of one of Hampton's own graduates.

104. Booker T. Washington.—Booker Taliaferro Washington was born about 1858 in Franklin County, Virginia. After the Civil War his mother and step-father removed to Malden, West Virginia, where when he became large enough he worked in the salt furnaces and the coal mines. He had always been called Booker, but it was not until he went to a little school at his home and found that he needed a surname that on the spur of the moment he adopted Washington. In 1872 he worked his way to Hampton Institute, where he paid his expenses by assisting as a janitor. Graduating in 1875, he returned to Malden and taught school for three years. He then attended for a year Wayland Seminary in Washington (now incorporated in Virginia Union University in Richmond), and in 1879 was appointed an instructor at Hampton. In 1881 there came to General Armstrong a call from the little town of Tuskegee, Ala., for some one to organize and become the principal of a normal school which the people wanted to start in that town. He recommended Mr. Washington, who opened the school on the 4th of

July in an old church and a little shanty, with an attendance of thirty pupils. In 1895 Mr. Washington came into national prominence by a remarkable speech at the Cotton States Exposition in Atlanta, and afterwards he interested educators generally by his emphasis on practical education. In 1896 the degree of Master of Arts was conferred on him by Harvard University, and that of Doctor of Laws by Dartmouth in 1901. He died November 14, 1915.

105. Message to the South.—The message which this man brought to the South, both to his own and to the white people, may best be expressed in his own words at the Atlanta Exposition : "To those of my race who depend on bettering their condition in a foreign land, or who underestimate the importance of cultivating friendly relations with the Southern white man who is their next door neighbor, I would say : 'Cast down your bucket where you are '—cast it down in making friends in every manly way of the people of all races by whom we are surrounded. . . . To those of the white race who look to the incoming of those of foreign birth and strange tongue and habits for the prosperity of the South, were I permitted I would repeat what I say to my own race, ' Cast down your bucket where you are.' Cast it down among the 8,000,000 Negroes whose habits you know, whose fidelity and love you have tested in days when to have proved treacherous meant the ruin of your firesides. . . . In all things that are purely social we can be as separate as the fingers, yet one as the hand in all things essential to mutual progress."

106. Significant Utterances.—It is of course hardly fair to represent any man by detached extracts from various addresses; at the same time it is possible to select from the speeches of Dr. Washington a few sentences which, taken together, may give a fairly adequate idea of his teaching and his gospel of work. Here are some such: " Freedom can never be given. It must be purchased." * " The race, like the individual, that makes itself indispensable, has solved most of its problems." * " As a race there are two things we must learn to do—one is to put brains into the common occupations of life, and the other is to dignify common labor." † " Ignorant and inexperienced, it is not strange that in the first years of our new life we began at the top instead of at the bottom; that a seat in Congress or the State Legislature was worth more than real estate or industrial skill." ‡ " The opportunity to earn a dollar in a factory just now is worth infinitely more than the opportunity to spend a dollar in an opera house." ‡ " One of the most vital ques-

* Speech before N. E. A. in St. Louis, June 30, 1904.
† Speech at Fisk University, 1895.
‡ Speech at Atlanta Exposition, Sept. 18, 1895.

tions that touch our American life, is how to bring the strong, wealthy, and learned into helpful contact with the poorest, most ignorant, and humblest, and at the same time make the one appreciate the vitalizing, strengthening influence of the other." * " There is no defense or security for any of us except in the highest intelligence and development of all." †

107. Tuskegee Institute.—The general expression of Dr. Washington's views about industrial education and the importance of the Negro's accumulating property and making himself respected, has been Tnskegee Normal and Industrial Institute. Beginning in 1881 with one teacher and only an annual grant of $2,000 from the Alabama Legislature, this school has developed until in 1917–18 it enrolled 1453 students with about 175 instructors, and possessed not less than 115 buildings constructed largely by student labor, and had about 40 industries in actual operation. In the academic department as well as in the industries, practical training is emphasized. One of the most important parts of Tuskegee is the Extension Work. This includes the well-known Annual Negro Conference; the Farmers' Monthly Institute; the Short Course in Agriculture; the Farm Demonstration work, now extended to Mississippi and Texas, and partly

* Speech at Harvard University, June 24, 1896.
† Speech at Atlanta Exposition.

supported by the United States Government; a town night school; a town afternoon cooking class; the County Institute; the Ministers' Night School; a weekly mothers' meeting; a state and county fair; and an occasional special conference, such as one on the Negro as a World Problem.

108. Offshoots.—The importance of the Tuskegee idea becomes manifest when it is seen that Tuskegee itself is not the only institution that in the way of practical education is touching the life of Negroes in the far South. More than fifteen similar schools have been established by Tuskegee graduates. These are widely scattered, typical ones being the Voorhees Industrial School, Denmark, S. C.; the Robert Hungerford School, Eatonville, Fla.; the Snow Hill Normal and Industrial Institute, Snow Hill, Ala.; the Utica Normal and Industrial Institute, Utica, Miss.; the Topeka Normal and Industrial Institute, Topeka, Kan.; the Port Royal Agricultural School, Beaufort, S. C.; and the Mt. Meigs Institute, Mt. Meigs, Ala.

109. National Negro Business League.—One typical organization will illustrate the influence of the Tuskegee idea. The National Negro Business League, of which Dr. Washington was the founder and first president, is in no way officially connected with Tuskegee Institute; yet it was conceived in the spirit of that institution and has adhered to its line of work. It was organized in 1899. There are now about 600 local leagues scattered throughout the country. When they began work there were only about half a dozen Negro banks in the country. There are now about 80. Dry goods stores, grocery stores, and industrial enterprises to the number of 15,000 have come into existence. Of course much of this progress would have been realized if the Negro Business League had never been organized; yet anyone must grant that in all this development the genius of the leader at Tuskegee has been the moving force.

CHAPTER XII

110. Conflicting Opinion and New Ideals.—The program advanced by Dr. Washington at once commanded attention; and the South, in the first flush of a new era of industrial development, and the North, for the time being interested mainly in the security of its Southern investments, both approved the new leader, who along the lines of thrift and self-reliance certainly gave tremendous inspiration to thousands of his fellowmen in the South. From the very first, however, there was a distinct group of Negro men who honestly questioned the ultimate wisdom of the so-called Atlanta Compromise. They felt that in seeming to be willing temporarily to accept segregation and to waive political rights Dr. Washington had given up too much. As the opposition, however, they were not at first united and constructive, and in their utterances they sometimes offended by harshness of tone. Dr. Washington himself said of the extremists in this group that they frequently understood theories but not things; that in college

they gave little thought to preparing for any definite
task in the world, but started out with the idea of preparing themselves to solve the race problem ; and that
many of them made a business of keeping the troubles,
wrongs, and hardships of the Negro race before the
public.* There was ample ground for his criticism.
More and more, however, the opposition gained force.
The *Guardian*, edited in Boston by Mr. Monroe Trotter, was particularly outspoken; the *Voice of the
Negro*, a monthly magazine published for three years
in Atlanta, helped toward the cultivation of racial
ideals; and in 1905 twenty-nine men of the race
launched what was known as the Niagara Movement.
The aims of this organization were freedom of speech
and criticism, an unlettered and unsubsidized press,
manhood suffrage, the abolition of all caste distinctions based simply on race and color, the recognition
of the principle of human brotherhood as a practical
present creed, the recognition of the highest and best
training as the monopoly of no class or race, a belief
in the dignity of labor, and united effort to realize
these ideals under wise and courageous leadership.
The time was not yet quite ripe and the Niagara Movement as such died after three or four years. Its principles lived on, however; nor did it pass before it had
definitely fixed attention upon a new leader, one who

* See chapter "The Intellectuals" in *My Larger Education*.

was more and more to prove himself a clear-voiced spokesman.

111. W. E. Burghardt DuBois.—William Edward Burghardt DuBois was born February 23, 1868, at Great Barrington, Mass. He received the degree of Bachelor of Arts at Fisk University in 1888, the same degree at Harvard in 1890, that of Master of Arts at Harvard in 1891, and, after a season of study at the University of Berlin, received also the degree of Doctor of Philosophy at Harvard in 1895, his thesis being his exhaustive study, *Suppression of the Slave-Trade.* Dr. DuBois taught for a brief period at Wilberforce University, and was also for a time an assistant and fellow in Sociology at the University of Pennsylvania, producing in 1899 his study, *The Philadelphia Negro.* In 1896 he accepted the professorship of History and Economics at Atlanta University, the position which he left in 1910 to become the Director of Publicity and Research for the National Association for the Advancement of Colored People. He has made various investigations, frequently for the national government, and has contributed many sociological studies to leading magazines. He has been the moving spirit in the Atlanta Conference, and by the Studies of Negro Problems which he has edited at Atlanta University he has become recognized as one of the great sociologists of the day, and as the man who more than anyone else has given scientific accuracy to studies relating to the Negro. Several books that he has written belong rather to our chapter on " Literature and Art." Just now we are concerned with his work in the larger life of the race and the nation.

112. National Association for the Advancement of Colored People.—The organization with which Dr. DuBois became identified in 1910 was begun by a group of men and women, without distinction as to race, who were so interested in the welfare of the Negro and indeed in the principles on which the country itself was founded, that they felt that the time had come for a simple declaration of human rights. The Association aims " to make 11,000,000 Americans physically free from peonage, mentally free from ignorance, politically free from disfranchisement, and socially free from insult." It had early in 1919 a membership of 50,000, its organ being the *Crisis*, a monthly magazine published in New York, with Dr. DuBois as editor. It wages a constant fight for justice in every way, has been singularly successful in placing before the public the evils of lynching, and it has widened the door of hope not only for the college man or woman, but for the agricultural laborer as well.

113. Racial Co-operation.—The National Association for the Advancement of Colored People is outstanding as an effort in co-operation between the races for the improvement of the condition of the Negro. Of special interest along the lines of economic betterment has been the work of the National League on Urban Conditions among Negroes, from whose headquarters in New York thousands of Negroes have been placed in honorable employment and the most cordial relations between these workers and their employers cultivated. Interesting also is the increasing concern of the young Southern college man about the problems at his very door. Special Phelps-Stokes fellowships for the study of problems relating to the Negro have been founded at the Universities of Virginia and Georgia, it is expected that similar fellowships will be founded in other institutions, and the new interest and activity are represented in a wider way by the annual meetings of the Southern Sociological Congress and the University Commission on Southern Race Questions. The Commission, organized in 1912, was established with the intention that it " should consult with leading men in both races, should endeavor to keep informed in regard to the relations existing between the races, and should aim especially to influence Southern college men to approach the subject with intelligent information and with sympathetic interest." The results of the first few years of such work have been noteworthy. Already seven or eight thousand young Southern men and women are regularly engaged in the study of the Negro, and from them work of increasing scholarship and social value may not unreasonably be expected.

114. Migration.—Very soon after the beginning of the great war in Europe in 1914 there began what will ultimately be known as the most remarkable migratory movement in the history of the Negro in America. The sudden ceasing of the stream of immigration from Europe created an unprecedented demand for labor in the great industrial centers of the North, and business men were not long in realizing the possibilities of a source that had as yet been used in only the slightest degree. Special agents undoubtedly worked in some measure; but the outstanding feature of the new migration was that it was primarily a mass movement and not one organized or encouraged by any special group of leaders. Those who left their homes in the South to find new ones in the North worked first of all in response to a new economic demand. Prominent in their thought to urge them on, however, were the generally unsatisfactory conditions in the South from which they had so long suffered and from which all too often there had seemed to be no escape. It is a very conservative estimate to say that in the four years 1915–18 not less than 500,000 Negroes thus changed their place of abode. Naturally in such a number many ignorant and unskilled persons were to be found, but sometimes the most skilled artisans and the most thoughtful owners of homes in different communities sold their property and moved away. These people sometimes were employed by the thousands by great industrial organizations. Not unnaturally, however, such a shifting of population did not take place without some inconvenience and hardship. In Pittsburgh and Philadelphia congestion in housing conditions became so great as to demand immediate attention. In more than one place moreover there were outbreaks in which lives were lost. The feeling in East St. Louis, Ill., accounted for one of the most depressing occurrences in the whole history of the race in America. For years this city had been an important industrial center. In the summer of 1915 a strike on the part of 4,500 white men in the packing plants led to the calling in of Negroes from the South, and by the spring of the next year perhaps as many as ten thousand had recently arrived in the city. Riots occurred in May. On July 2, however, there began a massacre in which hundreds of thousands of dollars of property were destroyed, six thousand Negroes driven from their homes, and about one hundred and fifty shot, burned, hanged, or maimed for life. Constituted officers of the law failed to do their duty, and the testimony of victims as to the torture inflicted upon them was such as to send a thrill of horror through the heart of the American people. In various ways, however, different earnest and noble-spirited organizations labored in the work of the adjustment of the Negro to his new condition. Representative of such effort was that of the Detroit branch of the National League on Urban Conditions among Negroes. This agency was not content with merely finding vacant positions, but approached manufacturers of all kinds through distribution of literature and by personal visits, and within twelve months was successful in placing not less than one thousand Negroes in employment other than unskilled labor. It also established a bureau of investigation and information regarding housing conditions, and generally aimed at the proper moral and social care of those who needed its service. The whole problem of the Negro laborer was of such commanding importance after the United States entered the war as to lead to the creation of a special Division of Negro Economics in the office of the Secretary of Labor. To the directorship of this was called Dr. George E. Haynes, Professor of Sociology and Economics at Fisk University, his special duties being to advise the Secretary and the directors of the several divisions on matters relating to Negro wage-earners, and to outline and direct plans for the greater co-operation of Negro workers with employers and other workers in agriculture and industries.

115. The Great War and the Negro.—When the United States entered the war in Europe in April, 1917, the question of overwhelming importance to the Negro people of course became that of their relation to the great conflict in which their country had become engaged. Their response to the draft call set a noteworthy example of loyalty to all other elements in the country. In the summer of 1917 interest centered especially upon the training of Negro officers at Camp Dodge, near Des Moines, Iowa. As many as 1,200 men became commissioned officers. The race furnished altogether to the fighting forces of the United States very nearly 400,000 men, of whom a little more than half saw service in Europe. Negro men served in all branches of the military establishment, cavalry, infantry, artillery (field and coast), signal corps, medical corps, aviation corps (ground section), ambulance and hospital corps, sanitary and ammunition trains, stevedore regiments, labor battalions, depot brigades, etc., and also served as regimental clerks, surveyors, and draftsmen. For the handling of many of the questions relating to these men, Mr. Emmett J. Scott was on October 1, 1917, appointed Special Assistant to the Secretary

of **War**. **Mr.** Scott had for a number of years assisted
Dr. Booker T. Washington as secretary at Tuskegee
Institute, and in 1909 he was one of the three members
of the special commission appointed by President
Taft for the investigation of Liberian affairs. His
work in his new office was to keep the Negro people
and the country at large fully informed as to the
policies of the Government aimed to benefit the Negro
soldiers, and to stimulate the patriotism of the Negro
people and vitalize their efforts to aid in the winning
of the war. Negro nurses were authorized by the
War Department for service in base hospitals at six
army camps—Funston, Sherman, Grant, Dix, Zachary
Taylor, and Dodge—and women served as canteen
workers in France and in charge of hostess houses in
the United States. Sixty Negro men served as chap-
lains; 350 as Y. M. C. A. secretaries; and others in
special capacities. Service of exceptional value was
rendered by Negro women in industries and on
farms; very largely also they maintained production
in mills and promoted the food supply through agriculture at the same time that they released men for
service at the front. Meanwhile the Negro people
at large were investing millions of dollars in Liberty
Bonds and War Savings Stamps and contributing
most generously to the Red Cross, Y. M. C. A., Y. W.
C. A., and other war relief agencies. In the summer of

1918 interest centered upon the actual performance of Negro soldiers in France and upon the establishment of units of the Students' Army Training Corps in twenty of the leading educational institutions of the race. When these units were demobilized in December, 1918, provision was made in a number of the schools for the formation of units of the Reserve Officers' Training Corps. In the whole matter of the war the depressing incident was the courtmartial of sixty-three members of the Twenty-fourth Infantry, U. S. A., on trial for rioting and the murder of seventeen people at Houston, Texas, August 23, 1917. The trial began November 1, 1917. As a result of it thirteen of the defendants were hanged December 11, forty-one sentenced to imprisonment for life, four to imprisonment for shorter terms, and five were acquitted. Negro soldiers at the front lived up to their great tradition of valor, and when the armistice was signed they were the American troops that were nearest the Rhine. Further detail of their actual achievement will be found in our next chapter, "The Negro as a Soldier."

116. Africa and the New Age.—As soon as the war was over and the period of readjustment had begun, the Negro became the subject of unusual attention, great emphasis being placed upon movements and meetings for the cultivation of better relations be-

tween the races in the South. The Negro people
themselves, however, while not less interested in their
own problems at home, suddenly awakened to a
very real concern for the future of the natives of
Africa, especially those whose destiny depended most
vitally upon the decisions of the Peace Conference
in Paris. In February, 1919, largely through the
personal effort of Dr. DuBois, a Pan-African Congress was held in Paris, the chief aims of which were the
hearing of statements on the condition of Negroes
throughout the world, the obtaining of authoritative
statements of policy toward the Negro race from the
Great Powers, the making of strong representations
to the Peace Conference sitting in Paris in behalf of
250,000,000 Negroes throughout the world, and the
laying down of principles upon which the future
development of the race must take place. At the
same time young Negro men in America began to
realize as never before their obligation to Africa and
the unparalleled opportunity for service offered by the
great continent. Thus the consideration of the history of the Negro in America passes into that of the
ultimate destiny of the Negro in Africa and the world.

CHAPTER XIII

THE NEGRO AS A SOLDIER

117. General Tribute.—The tributes that have been
paid to the courage and valor of the Negro American
soldier are many. The best of these is probably the
address of Dr. Booker T. Washington at the Chicago
Peace Jubilee, October 16, 1898, of which a Chicago
newspaper said that it contained one of the most elo-
quent tributes ever paid to the loyalty and valor of
the colored race, and at the same time was one of the
most powerful appeals for justice to a race which has
always chosen the better part. As generally representative of what has been said, we may accept the
words of a correspondent of the *Atlanta Journal* written near the end of July, 1898, with reference to the
conduct of Negroes in the Spanish-American War:
"Physically the colored troops are the best men in the
army, especially the men in the Ninth and Tenth
Cavalry. Every one of them is a giant. The Negroes
in the Twenty-fourth and Twenty-fifth Infantry, too,
are all big fellows. . . . The Negroes seemed to be
absolutely without fear, and certainly no troops ad-

vanced more promptly when the order was given than they."

118. Heroism in the Revolutionary War.—It is impossible within our limits to take note of all the Negroes who have in one way or another especially distinguished themselves in the wars of the United States. Only the foremost figures can receive attention. On March 5, 1770, occurred the Boston Massacre, occasioned by the conduct of some British soldiers who were arrogantly marching through State Street. An attack of some citizens upon these soldiers was led by Crispus Attucks, a runaway slave, who was a very tall and commanding figure. When the English troops fired, Attucks and three of the citizens were killed, the Negro being the first man to die. The Attucks Monument on Boston Common commemorates the deed. At the Battle of Bunker Hill, when Major Pitcairn of the British army was exulting in his expected triumph, Peter Salem, a Negro, rushed forward, shot him in the breast, and killed him. When Colonel Barton of the American army undertook to capture General Prescott while the royal army was stationed at Newport, R. I., his chief assistant—the man who really captured Prescott in bed—was a Negro named Prince.

119. The War of 1812.—In the War of 1812 "New York authorized the raising of two regiments of 'freedmen of color'—to receive the same pay and allowance as whites—and provided that 'any able-bodied slave' might enlist therein 'with the written consent of his master or mistress,' who was to receive his pay aforesaid, while the Negro received his freedom, being manumitted at the time of his honorable discharge." * While General Andrew Jackson was in command at Mobile, some American troops that had charged the British were retreating in disorder when a Negro named Jeffreys saved the day by placing himself at the head of the troops and rallying them to the charge. In preparing for the defense of New Orleans, Jackson called on the Negroes for assistance, and on December 18th he addressed to them words of commendation, in part as follows: "Soldiers: From the shores of Mobile I collected you to arms. I invited you to share in the perils and to divide the glory with your white countrymen. I expected much from you, for I was not uninformed of those qualities which must render you so formidable to an invading foe. I knew that you could endure hunger and thirst and all the hardships of war. I knew that you loved the land of your nativity, and that, like ourselves, you had to defend all that is most dear to man. But you have surpassed all my hopes. I have found in you, united to these qualities, that noble enthusiasm which impels

* Alexander, 333.

to great deeds." The Negroes were especially distinguished for their conduct at the Battle of New Orleans. About four hundred were in the engagement, and one of them gave Jackson the suggestion for his famous cotton breastworks. The conduct of the Negro in the navy may be seen from the statement by Commodore Chauncey in a letter to Captain Perry to the effect that he had fifty Negroes on his ship and that they were among his best men.

120. Heroism in the Civil War.—In the Civil War the Negro troops were especially distinguished for their heroism at Port Hudson, Fort Wagner, Fort Pillow, and around Petersburg. Some important operations culminated on July 8, 1863, in the capture of the Confederate batteries at Port Hudson, a small village on the left bank of the Mississippi River, about 135 miles above New Orleans. A Negro regiment under Colonel Nelson was prominent in the operations of the siege on May 27th. To it was assigned the task of taking an almost impregnable fort. The Negro soldiers could not possibly succeed, because a bayou that they had to cross was too deep; still they made seven desperate charges, for this was one of their very first opportunities in the war and their valor was being tested. Said the New York *Times* of the battle: "General Dwight, at least, must have had the idea not only that they (the Negro troops) were men, but something more than men, from the terrific test to which he put their valor. . . . Their colors are torn to pieces by shot, and literally bespattered by blood and brains. . . . One black lieutenant actually mounted the enemy's works three or four times, and in one charge the assaulting party came within fifty paces of them." * This was the occasion on which Color-Sergeant Anselmas Planciancois said before a shell blew off his head, "Colonel, I will bring back these colors to you on honor, or report to God the reason why." On June 6th the Negroes again distinguished themselves and won friends by their bravery at Milliken's Bend. The 54th Massachusetts, commanded by Colonel Robert Gould Shaw, was conspicuous in the attempt to take Fort Wagner, on Morris Island near Charleston, July 18, 1863. The regiment had marched two days and two nights through swamps and drenching rains in order to be in time for the assault. In the engagement nearly all the officers of the regiment were killed, among them Colonel Shaw. The picturesque deed was that of Sergeant William H. Carney, who seized the regiment's colors from the hand of a falling comrade and planted the flag on the works, and who, when borne bleeding and mangled off the field, said, "Boys, the old flag never touched the ground." Fort Pillow, a position on the Missis-

* Quoted from Williams, II, 321.

sippi, about fifty miles above Memphis, was when attacked April 13, 1864, garrisoned by 557 men, 262 of whom were Negroes. The fort was taken by the Confederates, but the feature of the engagement was the stubborn resistance offered by the Union troops in the face of great odds. In the Mississippi Valley, and in the Department of the South, the Negro had now done excellent work as a soldier. In the spring of 1864 he made his appearance in the Army of the Potomac. Around Richmond and Petersburg in July, 1864, there was considerable skirmishing between the Federal and the Confederate forces. Burnside, commanding a corps composed partly of Negroes, dug under a Confederate fort a trench a hundred and fifty yards long. This was filled with explosives, and on July 30th the match was applied and the famous crater formed. Just before the explosion the Negroes had figured in a gallant charge on the Confederates. The plan was to follow the eruption by an even more formidable charge, in which Burnside wanted to give his Negro troops the lead. A dispute about this and a settlement by lot resulted in the awarding of precedence to a New Hampshire regiment. Said General Grant later of the whole unfortunate episode: "General Burnside wanted to put his colored division in front; I believe if he had done so it would have been a success." With reference to the Negro and his conduct at home during the

Civil War, no words better sum up his position than those of Dr. Washington: "When the long and memorable struggle came between union and separation, when he knew that victory on one hand meant freedom, and defeat on the other his continued enslavement, with a full knowledge of the portentous meaning of it all, when the suggestion and temptation came to burn the home and massacre wife and children during the absence of the master in battle, and thus insure his liberty, we find him choosing the better part, and for four long years protecting and supporting the helpless, defenseless ones entrusted to his care."

121. The Spanish-American War.—There are four regiments of colored regulars in the army of the United States, the Twenty-fourth Infantry, the Twenty-fifth Infantry, the Ninth Cavalry, and the Tenth Cavalry. These fought during the last years of the Civil War, and entered the regular service in 1866. These regiments formed part of the force of the Americans in the Santiago campaign. Various volunteer companies were raised in Alabama, Virginia, Illinois, Indiana, Kansas, and Ohio. The eighth Illinois was officered throughout by Negroes, J. R. Marshall commanding; and Brevet-Major Charles E. Young, a West Point graduate, was in charge of the Ohio battalion. The very first regiment ordered to the front when the war broke out in 1898 was the

Twenty-fourth Infantry; and Negro troops were conspicuous in the fighting around Santiago. They
figured in a brilliant charge at Las Quasimas on
June 24th, and in an attack on July 1st upon a garrison at El Caney (a position of importance for securing
possession of a line of hills along the San Juan River,
a mile and a half from Santiago) the First Volunteer
Cavalry (Colonel Roosevelt's "Rough Riders") was
practically saved from annihilation by the gallant
work of the men of the Tenth Cavalry. Fully as
patriotic, though in another way, was the deed of the
Twenty-fourth Infantry. A yellow fever hospital
was to be cleansed and some victims of the disease
nursed. Learning that General Miles desired a regiment for this work, the Twenty-fourth volunteered
its services. By one day's work the men had succeeded in clearing away the rubbish and in so cleaning
the camp that the number of cases was greatly reduced.

122. Brownsville.—In 1906 occurred an incident
affecting the Negro in the army that received an extraordinary amount of attention in the public press.
In August, 1906, Companies B, C, and D of the
Twenty-fifth Regiment United States Infantry were
stationed at Fort Brown, Brownsville, Texas. On the
night of the 13th took place a riot in which one citizen
of the town was killed, another wounded, and the

chief of police injured. The people of the town accused the soldiers of causing the riot; and on November 9th President Roosevelt dismissed "without honor" the entire battalion, disqualifying its members for service thereafter in either the military or the civil employ of the United States. When Congress met in December Senator Foraker of Ohio placed himself at the head of the critics of the President's action; and on January 22nd the Senate authorized a general investigation of the whole matter, a special message from the President on the 14th having revoked the civil disability of the discharged soldiers. The case was finally disposed of by a congressional act approved March 3, 1909. The full text of this important act reads as follows:

"*Be it enacted by the Senate and House of Representatives of the United States of America in Congress assembled*, That the Secretary of War is hereby authorized to appoint a court of inquiry, to consist of five officers of the United States Army, not below the rank of colonel, which court shall be authorized to hear and report upon all charges and testimony relating to the shooting affray which took place at Brownsville, Texas, on the night of August thirteenth–fourteenth, nineteen hundred and six. Said court shall, within one year from the date of its appointment, make a final report, and from time to time shall make partial reports, to the Secretary of War of the results of such inquiry, and such soldiers and non-commissioned officers of Companies B, C, and D, of the Twenty-fifth Regiment United States Infantry, who were discharged from the military service as members of said regiment, under the provisions of Special Orders, Numbered Two hundred and sixty-six, dated at the War Department the ninth day of November, nineteen hundred and six, as said court shall find and report as qualified for re-enlistment in the Army of the United States shall thereby become eligible for re-enlistment.

" Sec. 2. That any noncommissioned officer or private who shall be made eligible for re-enlistment under the provisions of the preceding section shall, if re-enlisted, be considered to have re-enlisted immediately after this discharge under the provisions of the special order hereinbefore cited, and be entitled, from the date of his discharge under said special order, to the pay, allowances, and other rights and benefits that he would have been entitled to receive according to his rank from said date of discharge as if he had been honorably discharged under the provisions of said special order and have re-enlisted immediately."

123. Carrizal.—It was seven years after the Brownsville incident that once more, at an unexpected moment, the loyalty and heroism of the Negro soldier impressed the American people. Once more the tradition of Fort Wagner was preserved and passed on. The expedition of American forces into Mexico in 1916, with the political events attending this, is a long story. The outstanding incident, however, was that in which two troops of the Tenth Cavalry engaged. Said the *Review of Reviews* in reporting the occurrence: "The unfortunate occurrence at Carrizal on June 21 involves questions of fact upon which we are not prepared to express an opinion. About eighty colored troopers from the Tenth Cavalry had been sent a long distance away from the main line of the American army, on some such ostensible errand as the pursuit of a deserter. The situation being as it was, it might well seem that this venture was highly imprudent. At or near the town of Carrizal, our men seem to have chosen to go through the town rather than around it, and the result was a clash which resulted in the death of Captain Boyd, who commanded the detachment, and some twenty of his men, twenty-two others being taken prisoners by the Mexicans. According to Mexican accounts, our troops made the attack; according to reports of our own men, the Mexicans set a trap and opened fire. Meanwhile all other phases of the Mexican problem seemed for the moment to have been forgotten at Washington in the demand for the release of the twenty-two men who had been captured. There was of course no reason for holding them, and they were brought up to El Paso within a few days and sent across the line." Thus, though "some one had blundered," these men still did their duty. " Theirs not to make reply; theirs but to do and die." So in the face of odds they fought like heroes and lay dead beneath the Mexican stars.

124. The Great War in Europe.—The remarkable record made by the Negro in the previous wars of the country was fully equalled by that in the recent Great War. Negro soldiers fought with special distinction in the Argonne Forest, at Chateau Thierry, in Belleau Wood, in the St. Mihiel district, in the Champagne sector, at Metz, Vosges, etc., winning the highest praise from their French and American commanders. Entire regiments of Negro troops were cited for exceptional valor and decorated with the French Croix de Guerre—the 369th, the 371st, and the 372d; while groups of officers and men of the 365th, the 366th, the 368th, the 370th, and the first battalion of the 367th were also decorated. At the close of the war the highest Negro officers in the army were Colonel Charles Young (retired), on special duty at Camp Grant, Ill., Colonel Franklin A. Dennison, of the 370th Infantry, formerly the Eighth Illinois; and Lieutenant Colonel Benjamin O. Davis, of the Ninth Cavalry. Interest attaches to Colonel Davis as the highest Negro officer in active service in the regular army of the United States. Of Colonel Dennison the New York *Evening Post* said: " He has the distinction of being Colonel of the only Negro regiment officered entirely by soldiers of that race." This organization was the first American regiment stationed in the St. Mihiel sector; it was one of three that occupied a sector at Verdun when a penetration there would have been disastrous to the Allied cause; and it went direct from the training camp to the firing line. Especially noteworthy was the record of the 369th Infantry, formerly the Fifteenth Regiment, New York National Guard. This organization of fighters, in addition to having 191 of its members cited for valorous deeds performed in action, was also decorated as a unit, as has been said. At one period it was under shellfire for 191 days, and it held one trench for 91 days without relief. It was the first unit of Allied fighters to reach the Rhine, going down as an advance guard of the French army of occupation. A prominent hero in this regiment was Sergeant Henry Johnson, who returned with the Croix de Guerre with one star and one palm. He is credited with routing a party of Germans at Bois-Hanzey in the Argonne on May 5, 1918, with singularly heavy losses to the enemy. Of such quality was the Negro soldier in battle. Hardly less heroic was the sturdy service of stevedore regiments, or of the thousands of men in the army who did not go to France but who did their duty as they were commanded at home. The testimony of those who could speak authoritatively more than justified the reputation of the Negro soldier for valor. General Vincenden, the French commanding officer, said of the men of the 370th: " Fired by a noble ardor, they go at times even beyond the objectives given them by the higher command; they have always wished to be in the front line." General Duplossis saluted " the brave American (Negro) regiments that rivalled in intrepidity their French comrades." On the occasion of their leaving France, General Coybet said to the 371st and 372d that had been brigaded with the 157th French Division: " For seven months we have lived as brothers-at-arms, partaking of the same activities, sharing the same hardships and the same dangers. Side by side we took part in the great Champagne Battle, which was to be crowned by a tremendous victory. Never will the 157th Division forget the indomitable dash, the heroic rush of the American (Negro) regiments up the observatory ridge and into the Plain of Monthois. The most powerful defenses, the most strongly organized machine gun nests, the heaviest artillery barrages—nothing could stop them. These crack regiments overcame every obstacle with a most complete contempt for danger. Through their steady devotion the Red Hand Division (157th French) for nine whole days of severe struggle was constantly leading the way for the victorious advance of the Fourth Army. Officers, non-commissioned officers and men, I respectfully salute our glorious comrades who have fallen, and I bow to your colors—side by side with this—the flag of the 333d Regiment of Infantry (French). They have shown us the way to victory. Dear Friends from America, when you reach the other side of the ocean, do not forget the Red Hand Division. Our brotherhood has been cemented in the blood of the brave, and such bonds will never be destroyed." *

* Order No. 245, quoted by Dr. DuBois in the *Crisis*, March, 1919.

CHAPTER XIV

THE NEGRO CHURCH *

125. Sorcery.—Negro slaves brought with them from Africa to America a strong tendency toward nature worship and belief in witchcraft. Some had a vague conception of a supreme being, and here and there may have been found a Mohammedan or a Christian. Some native priests were transported; others assumed the functions of priests, and soon a degraded form of African religion and witchcraft appeared in the West Indies. From this developed the Voodooism † whose effect is still directly traceable in many parts of the United States. The older and more crafty priests possessed some skill in medical or poisonous plants which well qualified them for imposition upon the weak and credulous. These sorcerers threw a veil of mystery over their incantations

---

* This chapter is largely, but not wholly, based upon the valuable Atlanta Conference study, *The Negro Church*, edited by Dr. DuBois. Quotation marks generally refer to this publication; but in many places where it has not been possible so directly to give credit, the study is the source of the information.

† *Voodoo* or *Hoodoo* is from *Vaudois*, the French form of the name of Peter Waldo.

and plied an exceedingly lucrative trade. Ultimately the whole system, which at first had some basis in real religion, developed into mere imposture. Although slavery in America destroyed completely almost every spontaneous social movement among the Africans, the Negro priest became an important figure on the plantation, and "found his function as the interpreter of the supernatural, the comforter of the sorrowing, and as the one who expressed rudely, but picturesquely, the longing and disappointment and resentment of a stolen people." From such beginnings rose and spread the Negro Church; and in course of time it not unnaturally became the center of amusement and economic activity as well as of religion.

126. Beginnings of the Negro Church.—Early Negro churches came into being in one of the following ways: (1) As the result of special missionary effort; (2) As the result of discrimination against Negroes during divine worship; (3) As the natural sequence of unusually large congregations; and (4) As the expression of the preference of the Negro communicants themselves. The Moravians, or United Brethren, were the first who formally attempted the establishment of missions for Negroes, but these were not very successful. The Presbyterians began work in 1735. Methodism was introduced in New York in 1766 and almost from the first it made converts among the

Negroes. At any rate there were in 1786, among the regular members of Methodist churches in this country, 1,890 Negroes, and four years later the number had increased to 11,682. Not unnaturally, however, the Baptist denomination, being extremely democratic, established the first distinctively Negro churches. There has been much discussion as to which was the very first Negro Baptist church. Common acceptance long supported the claim of the First Bryan Baptist Church, of Savannah, founded by Andrew Bryan January 20, 1788.* It appears that in 1832 the larger part of the congregation left this church and formed what is now the large First African Baptist Church of Savannah. The most recent student † of the subject, however, has shown not only that there was a distinctively Negro Baptist church in Savannah as early as 1779–82, but that there was a Negro Baptist church at Silver Bluff ("on the South Carolina side of the Savannah River, in Aiken County, just twelve miles from Augusta, Ga.") founded "not earlier than 1773, not later than 1775." Another investigator ‡ has placed the first organization in Williamsburg, Va., in 1776. The St. Thomas Episcopal

---

* See James M. Simms, *The First Colored Baptist Church in North America.*

† Walter H. Brooks: *The Silver Bluff Church.*

‡ John W. Cromwell in *The Negro Church*, 30–37.

Church in Philadelphia was organized in 1791; Bethel Church in Philadelphia in 1794, and the Zion Methodist Church in 1796.

127. Early Preachers.—Some remarkable men were instrumental in these beginnings. Easily foremost was Richard Allen, father of African Methodism. Born a slave, this man was licensed to preach in 1782, and in 1816 at the General Conference of the African Methodist churches in Philadelphia, he was elected their first bishop. As an organizer he possessed talents of the highest order. He was actively identified with every forward movement among Negroes, irrespective of denomination, and was one of the promoters of the first national convention of Negroes ever held in the United States, that in Philadelphia in 1830. Associated with Allen at first was Absalom Jones, who, serving later at St. Thomas, became the first Negro Episcopal rector in the United States. Prominent also was John Gloucester, of Kentucky, the first Negro Presbyterian minister. This man was distinguished by his rich musical voice, and himself became the father of four Presbyterian ministers. Foremost among the early Negro Baptists was Lott Carey, of Virginia, a man of massive and erect frame, with the bearing of a prince. Born a slave in 1780, Carey worked for some years in a tobacco factory in Richmond, leading a wicked life. Converted in 1807, he made rapid advance in scholarship, was licensed to preach, organized the first missionary society in the country, and then went himself as a missionary to the colony of Liberia.

128. Baptists.—It is now time to attempt to review the progress made by the different religious denominations among Negroes. The Baptists now number 2,500,000. All but a very few are what are known as Regular Baptists. These people hold that as the church is a spiritual institution, membership and baptism should be confined to believers, among whom of course infants cannot be included. They also maintain that baptism should be by immersion, and their doctrine of congregational independence is held to render unnecessary any general creed, though it is assumed that their ministers accept the principles of liberty of conscience and of the divine authority of Scripture. The first state convention of Negro Baptists was organized in North Carolina in 1866; others soon followed. In 1880 the Negro Baptists withdrew from their white brethren in missionary enterprises, and organized in Montgomery their own national convention. The most remarkable result of their united efforts has been the Home Mission work, including the National Baptist Publishing Board in Nashville, which was organized in 1895 and which now publishes almost all of the literature used in Negro

Baptist churches and Sunday-schools. From Pennsylvania throughout the South weekly newspapers are published in interest of the denomination. Among the more prominent of these are the *Christian Banner* in Philadelphia, the *Georgia Baptist* in Augusta, Ga., and the *American Baptist* in Louisville. Negro Baptists, having such a large and varied membership as they possess, are generally representative of the advance of Negroes in the United States. While a great many of the most intelligent leaders of the race belong to the denomination, much yet remains to be done for the education of its ministry; and the large influence of the Baptist minister and his close contact with the masses make his education of the highest importance in any consideration of questions relating to the Negro.

129. Methodists.—Because of some important divisions in the church, the history of the Methodists is slightly more complicated than that of the Baptists. In 1816 a number of Negroes under the leadership of Richard Allen organized in Baltimore the African Methodist Episcopal Church. They withdrew from the parent body, the Methodist Episcopal Church, in order that they might have more freedom of action among themselves than they believed they could secure in continued association with their white brethren. Allen became their first bishop. As early as 1793–4 this man had purchased a lot near the corner of Sixth and Lombard streets in Philadelphia for the erection of the first Negro Methodist church in the country. "In doctrine, government, and usage, this church does not differ from the body from which it sprang. It has an itinerant and a local or non-itinerant ministry, and its territory is divided into annual conferences." It did not meet with a large measure of success until the close of the Civil War made it possible for it to extend its activities into the Southern states. Pennsylvania, however, was not the only state in which Negro Methodists revolted from the parent organization. In 1820 a union of churches in and near New York resulted in the formation of what is known as the African Methodist Episcopal Zion Church. The polity of this organization is slightly different from that of the A. M. E. Church. In it representation of the laity has been a prominent feature. "Laymen are in its annual conferences as well as in its general conferences, and there is no bar to the ordination of women." In 1844, because of the increasing difference between the North and the South on the subject of slavery, there was a division in the main body of the Methodist Episcopal Church, and the Methodist Episcopal Church, South, resulted. Considerable work for the Negroes was done by this latter organization before the Civil War, the distinctively Negro bodies not then being able to advance in the South. When the war was over, however, and the way was clear for them, the Methodist Episcopal Church, South, observed a great deflection of its Negro communicants to the A. M. E. and the A. M. E. Z. churches. Accordingly it deemed it wise to establish in 1870 its own Negro branch; and thus came into being the Colored Methodist Episcopal Church. All along a great many Negroes remained in the parent body, the Methodist Episcopal Church, whose missionary activity, we remember, led to the formation of the Freedmen's Aid Society. Although there are now other small branches of Negro Methodists, such as the African Union Methodist Protestants and the Congregational Methodists, the great majority of them belong to the four organizations already considered, the M. E., A. M. E., A. M. E. Z., and C. M. E. churches. In 1918 articles were drawn up looking to the organic union of the A. M. E., A. M. E. Z., and C. M. E. churches by the year 1925 under the denominational title of the United Methodist Episcopal Church. The combined membership of the Methodist denominations is more than 2,000,000. The A. M. E. Church is largest, having, with the inclusion of 100,000 probationers, just about 850,000 members. Its organ is the *Christian Recorder* of Philadelphia, the oldest Negro periodical in the United States. This was started, though under a different name, as early as 1848. The publishing department of the church also issues the *African Methodist Episcopal Review*, a publication of about 100 pages. The African Methodist Episcopal Church, however, is chiefly noteworthy on account of its Board of Bishops. A board of sixteen men more or less directly wield power over 900,000 American Negroes, and indirectly over two or more millions, administer $12,000,000 worth of property, and an annual budget of $600,000. These bishops are elected for life by a General Conference meeting every four years. They are men of striking appearance; probity and intelligence have always been in the ascendency among them, and the church has prospered. Next to the A. M. E. Church stands the A. M. E. Zion Church, with about 600,000 communicants. This church publishes a weekly paper, the *Star of Zion*, and a quarterly, the *African Methodist Episcopal Zion Review*. Negroes in the M. E. Church number 350,000, and in the C. M. E. Church 250,000. In the M. E. Church there has been an insistent demand for a Negro bishop; but although four missionary bishops to Africa have from time to time been elected, no Negro bishop for the church in the United States has yet been elected.

130. Presbyterians.—We turn now to the churches whose Negro membership is small in comparison with that of the large denominations already considered.

The Presbyterian Church, North, has contributed largely not only to the education of teachers and preachers, but also toward the maintenance in their work of preachers as well as teachers. The result has been a ministry whose average of intelligence is high. Congregations have been gathered and churches have been organized until now the Presbyterian Board has under its care at least 350 Negro churches and missions, with 21,000 members. On the ground, however, that conversions are comparatively few, it has recently been considering the advisability of curtailing its work. Also deserving of consideration is the Negro branch of the Cumberland Presbyterians, with a membership of about 13,000.

131. Congregationalists.—In England and the United States the Congregational denomination is an outgrowth of Puritanism. That it is not widely different in polity from the Baptist denomination is shown by the fact that in England in times of oppression it has always formed an alliance with this body of believers. Generally it emphasizes two principles: the independence of the local church with complete control of its concerns, and the fellowship of independent churches with one another in voluntary association. The denomination now numbers among Negroes about 15,000, and the membership is above the average in intelligence.

132. Episcopalians.—The Episcopal Church was the first American church to receive Negro members, but in spite of this fact the growth of that membership has been comparatively small. This was the one great Protestant church that did not split on the slavery question, with the result that for some years before and after the Civil War its Negro membership was a delicate subject. In recent years, however, especially by the appointment of capable men to positions of great responsibility, the church has exhibited toward the Negro an attitude about whose generosity there can be no question. In the country there are to-day very nearly one hundred Negro clergymen engaged in the work of the church, and these minister to about 25,000 Negro communicants. This membership is in general of unusual intelligence and in a few of the very large cities of the East there are to be found congregations of noteworthy importance. St. Philip's in New York, with its strength and culture, is generally representative of the larger churches.

133. Roman Catholics.—It was in 1888 that the Roman Catholic Church appointed its first Negro priests in the United States. Since that date there have been several others. Within the last few years especially, the church has become very aggressive in its work among the Negro people, winning adherents

204 A SHORT HISTORY OF THE AMERICAN NEGRO

in many places in the South where it was practically
unknown before. It has established many schools
and in other ways put forth definite missionary effort.
As the number of Negro Roman Catholics in the
United States is at present growing very fast, figures
are constantly changing; but the total membership
is hardly less than 250,000.

134. Summary.—Even from this brief review of the
Christian church as this has been effective among the
Negroes of the United States, it is to be observed that
there were early tendencies toward race segregation.
Later on there were tendencies toward race co-operation, and unfortunately but almost inevitably, there
was some friction with the missionary boards of the
great and long-established denominations. Standing
out in special prominence is the African Methodist
Episcopal Church, up to the present time the greatest
single achievement of the race in organization; and
noteworthy as an effort in racial co-operation and up-
building is the movement for the bringing together
of the different Negro Methodist denominations. A
feature also of the work of recent years has been the
rapid advance of the Roman Catholic Church. The
Baptist denomination is still much the largest in numbers, and before it and the other large denominations
opens a future of opportunity that one can only hope
will be worthy of the noble traditions of the past.

CHAPTER XV

135. The Beginnings.—As has already been seen in connection with the matter of the education of the Negro before the Civil War, in more than one place in what is now the Middle West private schools were organized and supported by manumitted Negroes who had gone thither several decades before the era of freedom. In 1838 there were in Philadelphia thirteen private pay schools for Negroes, several of these being taught by Negroes; and as early as 1835 one such school was opened by a Negro woman in New Orleans. Such efforts as these were praiseworthy, but they were of course disconnected and frequently short-lived. It was in connection with the churches that the principle of Self-Help in Negro Education received the best exemplification. Most of the first Negro schools were fostered by the churches, and many of the first Negro teachers were also preachers. Even to-day in the South church buildings are frequently used as school-

* As stated in the Preface, this chapter is largely drawn from the valuable pamphlet by Dr. R. R. Wright, Jr., published by the Committee of Twelve. Dr. Wright has very kindly consented that his study should be so used.

houses; and both the Baptists and the Methodists are doing aggressive educational work.

136. African Methodist Episcopal Schools.—The African Methodist Episcopal Church, which took the lead among Negroes in educational work, began its endeavors in this direction as early as 1844 with the purchase of 120 acres of land in Ohio for the Union Seminary, which was opened in 1847. In 1856 this church united with the Methodist Episcopal Church (North) in establishing in Greene County, Ohio, Wilberforce University, which in 1863 became the sole property of the A. M. E. Church. At the close of the Civil War the ministers of this church were sent to the South and were successful in organizing churches and schools. To-day they maintain twenty schools and colleges—one or more in each Southern state, two in Africa, and one in the West Indies. These had at last accounts over 200 teachers, 6,000 pupils, and school property valued at more than $1,200,000. The latest statistics show that Wilberforce is still the foremost of these institutions, and that other prominent ones are Morris Brown University, Atlanta, Ga.; Western University, Quindaro, Kan.; Allen University, Columbia, S. C.; Paul Quinn College, Waco, Texas, and Kittrell College, Kittrell, N. C. In a consideration of Self-Help on the part of Negroes the method of raising money for these schools is important. Each church has a local education society. The third Sunday in September is set apart as Education Day, when a general collection is taken in all the churches. In a recent year this amounted altogether to a little more than $51,000. Besides this, each member is taxed eight cents a year for the general education fund, which is reported at the annual conference. The total income from all sources for the educational work of the African Methodist Episcopal Church is not less than $150,000 a year.

137. Other Methodist Institutions.—The African Methodist Episcopal Zion Church operates twelve institutions, four of which are colleges, one a theological school, and seven secondary schools. There are 150 teachers with more than 4,000 students; and in a recent year more than $100,000 was raised by the church for educational work. The principal institution is Livingstone College, Salisbury, N. C. The Colored Methodist Episcopal Church, while it does not operate so many schools as the larger denominations, in proportion to its membership probably surpasses all other churches in exemplifying the principle of self-help. Its chief institutions are Lane College, Jackson, Tenn.; Miles Memorial College, Birmingham, Ala.; and the Mississippi Industrial College, Holly Springs, Miss. The church also contributes to the support of Paine College, Augusta, Ga. The African Methodist Protestant Church has three small schools. Negroes have also contributed in large measure to the support of Methodist Episcopal missionary schools; but for these of course it is impossible to arrive at definite statistics.

138. Baptist Schools.—The educational work of the Negro Baptists is still largely under the control of the American Baptist Home Mission Society, which owns and operates the foremost institutions. In recent years, however, there has been a widespread movement among Negro Baptists to do educational work independently. This has resulted in the founding of a large number of schools, altogether about 120. These are of course too many, and they range in efficiency all the way from a fairly well established institution like Selma University to a school operated by a small association. These institutions are frequently forced to take the place of public high schools, and almost without exception they are inadequately equipped. Their rapid development, however, is indicative of the spirit of self-help. Where there is such variety of status, accurate statistics are impossible; but all these schools taken together enroll about 30,000 students and employ about 700 teachers. Prominent institutions are: in Alabama, Selma University; in Arkansas, Arkansas Baptist College in Little Rock; in Florida, Florida Baptist College in Jacksonville, and Florida Institute in Live Oak; in Georgia, Americus Institute in Americus, Walker Baptist Institute in Augusta, Jeruel Academy in Aihens, and Central City College in Macon; in Kentucky, State University in Louisville; in South Carolina, Morris College in Sumter, and Seneca Institute in Seneca; in Texas, Guadaloupe College in Seguin, and Central Texas College in Waco; in Tennessee, Howe Institute in Memphis, and the new Roger Williams University in Nashville; and in Virginia, Virginia Seminary in Lynchburg. As nearly as can be estimated, the Negro Baptists in their churches alone raised for their educational work in 1907 $149,332.75. Aside from the eight schools considered in a former chapter, the American Baptist Home Mission Society contributes in a smaller degree to twenty other institutions. The word of the Secretary * of this organization may be taken as summing up what the Negro Baptists have done for themselves: "We are sometimes told that it is about time for the Negroes to do something toward their own education, and some members of our churches seem to believe that their missionary money boards and clothes the thousands of pupils in attendance at the twenty-eight schools of the Home Mission Society. The following facts entirely refute these assertions: During the ten years ending

* Dr. C. L. White, in the *Home Mission Monthly*, April, 1909.

March 31, 1907, pupils paid for tuition $300,517.62; for board $954,822.01, and Negro churches and individuals gave for the support of the work or for new buildings to supplement the gifts of their Northern friends, $197,995.70. This makes a total of $1,453,335.33 paid or given by the Negroes for ten years, or $145,333.53 annually. It should be remembered that this is only a small part of the vastly larger amount contributed by these people for education, for all through the South many associations have their own denominational schools, and sacrifices are made for their maintenance which reflect credit upon the race which is so rapidly coming forward. The Negro presidents and principals are showing unusual wisdom in collecting funds for their work. Negro churches, too, are taking a great interest in these mission schools. The gifts from the Home Mission Society are hastening the day of still larger efforts from those benefited."

139. Self-Help in the Public Schools.—As early as 1869 General Howard reported that the recently emancipated freedmen had in one year raised for the construction of schoolhouses and the support of teachers not less than $200,000. Since 1870 common school education has been conducted chiefly by states, and the Negroes' contributions have been mainly through taxes, though not exclusively so. Though there is no authoritative source from which may be

drawn accurate conclusions, it is very probable that
the Negroes have paid for the entire amount of public
school education which they have received from the
Southern states since 1870. This does not mean,
however, that the direct taxes on the property of the
Negroes have been sufficient to pay for their common
school education, for they have not. But neither have
the direct taxes on the property of the white people
been sufficient to pay for their common school education. In Georgia, when everything is considered, it
becomes evident that the Negroes are in no sense a
burden on the white taxpayers, and that although
they pay hundreds of thousands of dollars each year
to white people as rent for their real estate, they do
not receive one cent from the taxes on this property
for their education. What is true of Georgia is true of
every other Southern state. In 1889 the Superintendent of Public Instruction in North Carolina, ad-
dressing the school officers of the state, said: "Do you
know, that including the poll tax, which they actually
pay, fines, forfeitures, and penalties, the Negroes
furnish a large proportion of the money that is applied to their schools?" In 1900 the Superintendent
of Education of Florida wrote: "The education of the
Negro of Middle Florida does not cost the white
people of that section one cent. The presence of the
Negro has actually been contributing to the main-

tenance of the white schools. The schools for Negroes not only are no burden upon the white citizens, but $4,527.00 contributed for Negro schools from other sources was in some way diverted to the white schools." As late as 1904 moreover, Superintendent of Public Instruction Joyner of North Carolina showed in his annual report that the Negroes were "in no danger of being given more than they were entitled to by every dictate of justice, right, wisdom, humanity, and Christianity."

140. Negro Philanthropy.—The Negro race is yet poor. Already, however, there have been many individuals who have given considerable sums to education. Only a few, however, can be mentioned. Bishop Payne gave several thousand dollars to Wilberforce, and Wheeling Gant gave $5,000. From the estate of Mary E. Shaw Tuskegee received $38,000. In Baltimore Nancy Addison left $15,000 and Louis Bode $30,000 to the Community of Oblate Sisters of Providence. George Washington, of Jerseyville, Ill., a former slave, left $15,000 for the education of Negroes. There have been two gifts to education, however, that are remarkable because they were unusually large and because they were made by Negroes of whom the world at large knew but little until the time of their death. Thomy Lafon, of New Orleans, left $413,000 to charitable and educational institutions in that city, without distinction of color; and Col. John McKee, of Philadelphia, who died in 1902, left about a million dollars in real estate for education. Mme. C. J. Walker in 1919 also left bequests aggregating thousands of dollars.

141. Negro Teachers.—The first teachers of the Negroes were almost all white people. In 1867 the Freedmen's Bureau reported 1,056 Negro teachers, and in 1870 1,324. In 1908 nearly all the public schools for Negroes in the South were in the hands of Negro teachers, the great majority of whom were graduates of normal or high school courses in missionary institutions. In the colleges, as Negroes have become more and more efficient, the tendency has been to give them larger and larger responsibilities. In the Methodist Episcopal Church the Senior Secretary having charge of the schools of the Freedman's Aid Society is a Negro, and his organization has in recent years appointed several Negroes to the presidency of important schools. Twelve years ago the American Baptist Home Mission Society made the departure of promoting a Negro to the presidency of one of its chief institutions, Morehouse College; and more recently it has pursued a similar policy in the case of Jackson College. In Biddle University, the largest school of the Presbyterians, and the St. Paul Normal and Industrial School at Lawrenceville, Va., one of the most prominent institutions of the Episcopalians, Negro men have been given the conduct of affairs. The schools of the American Missionary Association have sometimes drawn their professors from the graduates of Negro institutions; but this organization has not yet followed the other large missionary societies in appointing a Negro to the presidency of one of its leading colleges. The A. M. E. and A. M. E. Zion schools have of course had Negro teachers all along; and Howard University has also had Negroes in important places since the beginning.

142. Conclusions.—In the light of what has been said we may make the following observations:—

1. It is probably true that the Negroes pay a larger percentage of the cost of their schools than any other group of poor people in America.

2. The Negroes have paid in direct property and poll-taxes more than $60,000,000 during the last fifty years.

3. The Negroes have contributed at least $24,000,000 to education through their churches.

4. The Negro student probably pays a larger percentage of the running expenses of the institutions which he attends than any other student in the land.

5. There are at present at work 32,000 Negro teachers, 20,000 ministers, and 400 newspapers and magazines and other agencies of self-help.

CHAPTER XVI

143. General Advance.—Within the period of a little more than half a century since emancipation the Negro race has advanced not only in home-life, in organization, and in art, but in almost every field of endeavor it has produced individuals whose achievement challenges consideration by the highest standards of American culture. In the list of professions and occupations one observes architects, chemists, metallurgists, designers, and other skilled workers in an ever-increasing number, and more and more have these people made themselves a necessary element in the civilization of which they are so vital a part. Along with general progress has gone increasing racial consciousness and pride. About five hundred men are now engaged in the work of journalism, and through such a magazine as the *Crisis* and such weekly newspapers as the *Age* (New York), the *Freeman* (Indianapolis), and the *Défender* (Chicago), the aspiration of the race finds expression; while the quarterly *Journal of Negro History* is representative of work in the higher fields of scholarship.

144. Home-Life and Health.—In no way perhaps has the general advance been better shown than in the improved conditions of home-life. In spite of inadequate hygienic facilities in many places, the Negro constantly shows a striving to make his home and his surroundings as comfortable and as refined as possible. By the census of 1910 the aggregate number of all homes occupied by Negro families in the Southern states was 1,917,391, of which 430,449, or 22.4 per cent, were reported as owned, including 314,340 reported as owned free of encumbrance. Within one decade a division of four states—Arkansas, Louisiana, Oklahoma, and Texas—showed an increase of 65 per cent in the ownership of homes other than farm houses; and one city in the 25,000 class, Petersburg, Va., before the recent war set the very high standard of one owned home for every 13 of its Negro inhabitants, and in the 10,000 class Greenville, Miss., had one owned home for every 11. In the North, where the Negro population is of course by no means as stable as in the South, much greater use is made of temporary abodes; thus in a crowded center like New York lodgers hardly ever number less than 30 per cent of the total Negro population. Closely connected with the whole subject of housing conditions of course is that of mortality. The figures here are depressing. In 57 representative cities in 1910 the death rate among Negroes was 27.8 per 1,000, as compared with 15.9 per 1,000 for the white people. However, every city in the South except two showed in 1910 a lower death rate than in 1900. On the other hand half of the cities in the North showed an increase in the death rate in 1910 over that of 1900. Very vital is the point that as the number of owned homes in a given area increases the mortality figures decidedly decrease. Evidently the whole matter of sanitation, with the securing of better light and water facilities and the furnishing of wholesome recreation, should be one of the chief concerns of those interested in the welfare of the race in America.

145. Organization and Business.—It is not only in his home-life that the Negro has learned to exhibit the virtues of thrift and self-reliance. In the wider field of organization and co-operation he is rapidly developing large enterprises. We have already remarked the National Negro Business League, founded in 1899. The annual meetings of this organization years ago became the rallying-place of many of the foremost business men of the race. Important also is the work of several strong fraternal and benefit organizations, and the last two decades have witnessed an interesting multiplication of insurance companies throughout the South. The African Methodist Episcopal Church has at Philadelphia an extensive publishing business in the A. M. E. Book Concern, and the Baptists have at Nashville the National Baptist Publishing Board. There are other church publishing firms, but these are the largest distinctively Negro enterprises. Among secular interests must be remarked the Mme. C. J. Walker Manufacturing Co. of Indianapolis and New York, whose business is now conducted in accord with the principles regularly governing large American commercial organizations.

146. Industry.—It is not only in his own industrial enterprises that the Negro is felt, however; upon his shoulders has fallen much of the most arduous and necessary work of the nation. In 1910, of 3,178,554 Negro men at work in the country, 981,922 were listed as farm laborers and 798,509 as farmers. That is to say, 56 per cent of the whole number were engaged in raising farm products either on their own account or by way of assisting somebody else. If to these are added men in the building and hand trades, saw and planing mills, as well as railway firemen and porters, draymen, teamsters, and coal mine operatives, it will be found that a total of 71.2 per cent were engaged in such work as represents the very foundation of American industry. Of the women 1,047,146, or 52 per cent, were either farm laborers or farmers, and 28 per cent more were either cooks or washer-women. In other words, a total of 80 per cent were

doing some of the hardest and at the same time some
of the most necessary work in American home and
industrial life. Under the influence of the migration
of 1915–18 Negro men were employed by the thousands in the great industrial centers of the North.
They gave a good account of themselves. On one
occasion Charles Knight, a Negro riveter of the
Bethlehem Steel Corporation at Sparrows Point, Md.,
drove 4,875 three-quarter rivets in a nine-hour day,
breaking the previous record by 433. He was
awarded the first international prize for riveting,
$125, offered by Lord Northcliff. Unfortunately the
general attitude of the labor unions in the North
has not always been cordial toward the Negro worker,
and the adjustment of this problem is one of the
most important questions in the whole range of the
industrial life of America.

147. Invention.—The first Negro scientist to come
into prominence was Benjamin Banneker of Maryland, who in 1770 constructed the first clock striking the hours that was made in America, and who
published annually from 1792 to 1806 an almanac
adapted to the requirements of Maryland and the
neighboring states. Banneker attracted much attention by his knowledge of mathematics and astronomy, and his achievements made a reputation for him
in Europe as well as in America. Up to the present

time there have been granted to Negroes a little more than 1,000 patents. The honor of being granted the first belongs to Henry Blair of Maryland, evidently a free Negro, who in 1834 took out a patent for a corn harvester. In ante-bellum days a rather queer situation arose more than once. If a slave made an invention he was not permitted to take out a patent, for no slave could make a contract; but neither could a slave's master take out a patent for him, for the Government would not recognize the slave as having the legal right to make the contract of assignment of his invention to his master. Within more recent years Granville T. Woods appears to have surpassed every other inventor of the race in the number and the variety of his inventions. His record began in 1884 in Cincinnati, Ohio, where he then resided, and continued without interruption until his death in New York in 1910. Among his inventions may be found valuable improvements in telegraphy, including a system for telegraphing from moving trains; also an electric railway and a phonograph. Many of his patents were assigned to such companies as the General Electric Company, of New York, and the American Bell Telephone Company, of Boston. The authority on the subject * says that there has been no inventor of the race " whose achievements have attracted more universal attention and favorable comment from technical and scientific journals both in this country and abroad " than those of Granville T. Woods. Elijah McCoy, of Detroit, Mich., who began his work as early as 1872, has been granted about fifty patents, relating particularly to lubricating appliances for engines. Many of his inventions have long been in use on the locomotives of the Canadian and Northwestern railroads, and on the steamships of the Great Lakes. Jan E. Matzeliger, a Dutch Guiana Negro born in 1852, came to this country as a very young man and served an apprenticeship as a cobbler first in Philadelphia and then in Lynn, Mass. His hardships undermined his health and he passed away in 1889 in the thirty-seventh year of his age, but not before he had invented a machine for attaching soles to shoes, " the first appliance of its kind capable of performing all the steps required to hold a shoe on its last, grip and pull the leather down around the heel, guide and drive the nails into place, and then discharge the completed show from the machine." The patent for this invention was bought by the president of the United Shoe Machinery Company

Colored Inventor," and he contributed "The Negro in the Field of Invention" to the *Journal of Negro History* for January, 1917. A book by him is expected.

of Boston, and Matzeliger's invention thus formed the basis of a great enterprise that represents the consolidation of forty subsidiary enterprises and that gives regular employment to thousands of people. J. H. Dickinson and his son, S. L. Dickinson, both of New Jersey, have been granted more than a dozen patents for their appliances, mainly in the line of devices connected with the machinery of the player piano. W. B. Purvis, of Philadelphia, has been granted more than a dozen patents having to do with machinery for the making of paper bags, many of these being sold to the Union Paper Bag Company, of New York. Benjamin O. Jackson, of Massachusetts, has been granted nearly as many patents for his inventions, including a heating apparatus, a gas burner, an electrotyper's furnace, and a trolley wheel controller; and many other men have invented devices hardly less interesting than those mentioned.

148. Professions and Public Life.—In the so-called learned professions—the Ministry, Law, and Medicine—the Negro has made rapid progress. In fact, if to these be added teaching, and, in later years, business, we shall have the fields upon which the race has primarily depended for its leadership. These professions are frequently thought to be crowded, and yet in 1910, of a total Negro population of more than 10,000,000, and of 3,178,554 men at work, only

17,427 were listed as clergymen, 3,077 as physicians and surgeons, 796 as lawyers, and 7,035 as teachers (169 others being specially listed as college presidents or professors). In this same year 22,450 women were schoolteachers; and within the last two decades women have made most noteworthy advance in all of the arts and professions. In individual cases they are outstanding, and numerically in music and the other arts the ratio of men to women is just about 3 to 2. Every one of the prominent denominations can furnish examples of men who are distinguished for eloquence, for community service, or for high spiritual leadership. In many communities where the church is the only social institution the preacher must still be the general adviser of the people in all of the ordinary affairs of life. To the lawyers also has naturally fallen much of the leadership of the race, especially in political affairs. With the large and pressing problems that have arisen in the social and civil life of the Negro within recent years this profession has received a new emphasis as one of the highest importance. Among those men who within recent years have been prominent in the public life of the nation have been Judson W. Lyons, William T. Vernon, and J. C. Napier as registers of the treasury of the United States; Charles W. Anderson as collector of internal revenue for the second district of New York; William

H. Lewis as assistant attorney general of the United States; and Emmett J. Scott, previously remarked, as special assistant to the Secretary of War.

149. Medicine.—The history of the Negro physician is one of unusual and special interest. Even in colonial times, though there was much emphasis on the control of diseases by roots or charms, there was a beginning in work genuinely scientific. In the earlier years of the last century James Derham, of New Orleans, became the first regularly recognized Negro physician of whom there is a complete record. About the middle of the century, in New York, James McCune Smith, a graduate of the University of Glasgow, was prominent. "The first real impetus to bring Negroes in considerable numbers into the professional world came from the American Colonization Society, which in the early years flourished in the South as well as in the North. This organization hoped to return the free Negroes to Africa and undertook to prepare professional leaders of their race for the Liberian colony. ' To execute this scheme, leaders of the colonization movement endeavored to educate Negroes in mechanic arts, agriculture, science, and Biblical literature. Exceptionally bright youths were to be given special training as catechists, teachers, preachers, and physicians. Not much was said about what they were doing, but now and then appeared notices of Negroes who had been prepared privately in the South or publicly in the North for service in Liberia. Dr. William Taylor and Dr. Fleet were thus educated in the District of Columbia. In the same way John V. DeGrasse, of New York, and Thomas J. White, of Brooklyn, were allowed to complete the medical course at Bowdoin in 1849. In 1854 Dr. DeGrasse was admitted as a member of the Massachusetts Medical Society.'"* Very prominent about this time was Martin R. Delany, of Pittsburgh, who, after being refused admission at a number of institutions, was admitted to the medical school at Harvard. He became distinguished for his work in a cholera epidemic in Pittsburgh in 1854 and in his later years was outstanding as a race leader. After the Civil War medical departments were established in several of the new institutions of learning. As they have developed, the School of Medicine at Howard University and the Meharry Medical College, Nashville, Tenn., have proved to be the strongest. In the period after the Civil War two physicians in the District of Columbia became especially prominent. One of these, A. T. Augusta, studied medicine at the University of Toronto and became the first Negro to hold a position

---

* Kelly Miller: "The Historical Background of the Negro Physician," *Journal of Negro History*, April, 1916, quoting in part C. G. Woodson: "The Education of the Negro Prior to 1861."

as surgeon in the United States Army. Charles B. Purvis, a graduate of the Medical College at Western Reserve University in Cleveland, also became a surgeon in the Army and was for a long period connected with the Freedmen's Hospital in Washington. He did more than any other man to develop the medical school at Howard.* At the present time the Negro physicians in the country number hardly less than 6,000 and the dentists very nearly 1,000.

150. Scholarship and Special Distinction.—Several students and investigators are at present engaged in original work in the field of medicine just remarked, and in chemistry, history, and social science as well. More and more these diligent workers are interpreting their pursuits in terms of regular academic standards, so that the number of those who have taken the degree of Doctor of Philosophy at the great universities of the country now number not less than twelve. Among those investigators who have best brought their work to bear upon the ordinary needs of life must be remarked Professor George W. Carver of Tuskegee Institute, whose general acquaintance with plants and whose breeding of new varieties of cotton and studies in the sweet potato and other foods have deservedly given him a national reputation. Dr. DuBois was outstanding in scholarship for several years

* Miller, as above.

before he became so prominent as a race leader; and
Dr. Carter G. Woodson as the editor of the *Journal
of Negro History* has given great impetus to study in
this field. In 1914 Dr. (now Major) Joel E. Spingarn
offered as an annual prize a bronze medal of the value
of $100 to be awarded to that man or woman who,
by his or her individual achievement as judged by a
committee, should have reflected most credit upon
the race in any honorable field of endeavor. In 1915
the first award of the Spingarn medal was made to
Dr. E. E. Just, a biologist and a professor in Howard
University. In 1916 it was awarded to Colonel (then
Major) Charles Young for his distinction in the public
service, especially in Liberia; in 1917 to Harry T.
Burleigh, the foremost musician of the race; in 1918
to William Stanley Braithwaite, the distinguished
critic and sponsor for American poetry; and in 1919
to Archibald H. Grimké, of Washington and Boston,
for his efforts in the public service extending over
several fields for a number of years.

CHAPTER XVII

151. Folk-Lore and Folk-Music.—In the life and history of the Negro people there has developed a large tradition of interesting customs, superstitions, and tales. Of the writers of the race Charles W. Chesnutt was the first who fully appreciated the literary value of this material; but other writers, such as Thomas Nelson Page and George W. Cable, have also found it of great service. Its chief literary monument so far has been in the Uncle Remus tales told by Joel Chandler Harris. Important as is Negro folklore, however, the folk-music of the race is still more so. Negro music in America is especially interesting because it is not only the voice of an uncivilized people in Africa, but also a highly developed folk-music. Dr. DuBois distinguishes four steps in its development. The first stage exhibits native African music, and may be seen in such a chant as that for the words, "You may bury me in the East;" the second is that of Afro-American music, the great class, "Steal away to Jesus" being an example; the third stage shows a blending of Negro music with that of the foster-land, as in "Bright Sparkles in the Churchyard;" the fourth shows American melodies affected by the Negro music, as in the songs of Stephen Collins Foster. Another division of the melodies makes two classes of them, those which are the spontaneous expression of the Negro's own feelings, and those which, while now essentially Negro in character, show some evidence of foreign origin. In the second group may be seen traces of European songs and dances, and adaptations of Baptist and Methodist hymns. Those songs which are altogether original are generally religious in tone and most often sorrowful. Typical ones are "My Lord, what a Morning" and "Nobody knows de trouble I've seen." Sometimes however the note of triumph sounds with tremendous force, as in "Oh, give way, Jordan," "In dat great gittin'-up mornin'," and "Oh, den my little soul's gwine to shine." No one is yet able to say just how many of these melodies are in existence, for they have not all been collected. Unlike the English and Scottish popular ballads, they depend for their merit vastly more upon their tunes than upon their words. They are also more affected by nature than are the ballads. A meteoric shower, a thunder-storm, or the dampness of a furrow was sufficient to give birth to a hymn, and the freest possible use was made of figures of speech. As in the ballads, the sentiment of the individual becomes universal; and there is a strong tendency toward repetition. The time-structure of the melodies has frequently astonished musicians by its accuracy; but in recent years there has been a decided tendency toward debasement. "Ragtime" depends for its effect upon an exaggeration of the "rhythmical snap" that is so prominent in Negro music, and upon an excessive use of syncopation. The distinction between "ragtime" and the pure "spirituals" should be insisted upon, however, and more and more should the current debasement of Negro music be discouraged.

152. Phillis Wheatley.—The first Negro to achieve distinction in literature in America was Phillis Wheatley. This young woman was born in Africa, in Senegal, in 1753 or 1754. When she was brought to America in 1761 she was bought for Mrs. Susannah Wheatley, wife of John Wheatley, a tailor, who desired to have a special servant for her declining years. The bright mind and delicate figure of the child soon distinguished her from the other slaves of the household; and with the assistance of Mary Wheatley, the daughter of the family, Phillis learned to read. Within sixteen months from the time of her arrival in Boston she was able to read fluently the most difficult parts of the Bible; and gradually she came to be looked upon by Mrs. Wheatley as a daughter or companion rather than a slave. In course of time the learning of the young student came to consist of a little astronomy, some geography, a little ancient history, a fair knowledge of the Bible, and a thorough and appreciative acquaintance with the most important Latin classics. Even these modest attainments were most rare for an American woman of the period. Phillis soon turned her attention to the composition of verses, using Pope's Homer as her model; and, as one critic has said, she "became a kind of poet laureate in the domestic circles of Boston." Not only did the gracious demeanor of the girl single her out for special favors at the hands of Mrs. Wheatley's friends; at the age of sixteen she became a member of the congregation of the Old South Meeting House, being the first slave to be admitted into that body. In 1773, after formal manumission, she went to England under the care of Nathaniel Wheatley, the son of the family, the thought being that the air of the sea would improve her health. While abroad she was under the special patronage of the Countess of Huntingdon, to whom a poem on the death of George Whitefield, the former chaplain of this lady, had introduced her. By her wit and modesty she made many friends abroad; presents were showered upon her, Brook Watson, Lord Mayor of London, giving her a copy of a magnificent folio edition of *Paradise*

Lost, which is now in the library of Harvard College.
While she was in England arrangements were made
for the publication of her volume of verses, *Poems on
Various Subjects*. The illness of her old friend, Mrs.
Wheatley, caused her to hasten her return to America.
Mrs. Wheatley died in 1774, and her husband in 1778.
The daughter of the family, who had married and left
the old home, also died in 1778. Nathaniel Wheatley
was living abroad. In her loneliness Phillis listened
to the voice of John Peters, a ne'er-do-well variously
reported to have been a baker, a barber, a grocer, a
doctor, and a lawyer. She was married in April, 1778.
Hard times now came to her, and her health declined.
At last she was compelled to accept work as a drudge
in a cheap boarding-house. She became the mother
of three children. Two died before her, and her last
baby slept with its mother in death December 5, 1784.

Phillis Wheatley's collection, *Poems on Various
Subjects*, contains thirty-nine titles. Fourteen of the
thirty-eight original pieces are elegiac and not at all
remarkable for poetic merit; at least six others may
be classed as occasional; and two are mere paraphrases
of portions of the Bible. We are thus left with sixteen
poems which permit us to judge of the ability of
Phillis Wheatley. Let us keep in mind the fact that
all these pieces were written by a girl not yet twenty
years old. The masterpiece is undoubtedly *On Imag-*

ination, lines suffused with true poetic feeling. Several other poems are of interest for different reasons. *On Being Brought from Africa to America* consists of eight childish but sincere lines. *On Virtue* is the remarkable utterance of a pious, but fatherless and motherless, child. *To S. M., a Young African Painter, on Seeing his Works* was addressed to Scipio Moorhead, a young Negro who had evidently some talent for painting, and one of whose pictures (one infers from the poem) dealt with the story of Damon and Pythias.

The form of the verses shows decided imitation of Alexander Pope. The heroic couplet swings through all except two or three of the poems. The diction also is pseudo-classic. The earnestness of the work, however, is one of its strong assets. Phillis Wheatley is intensely serious and pious. She never intends to be humorous, and when in *To the University of Cambridge, in New England* the young girl of nineteen gives advice to the students at Harvard, it is not because she so intends that she provokes a smile.

As a woman Phillis Wheatley was eminently noble. Hers was a great soul. Her ambition knew no bounds, her thirst for knowledge was insatiable, and she triumphed over the most adverse circumstances. A child of the wilderness and a slave, by her grace and culture she satisfied the conventionalities of Boston and of London. Her brilliant conversation was equalled only by her modest demeanor. Everything about her was refined: her figure was delicately moulded; her handwriting was plain and neat. More and more as one studies her life he becomes aware of her sterling Christian character; and it was meet that the first Negro woman in American literature should be one of unerring piety and unbending virtue.

153. Paul Laurence Dunbar.—Dunbar was born June 27, 1872, in Dayton, Ohio. When he attended the Steele High School in Dayton he edited *The High School Times*, a monthly student publication, and when he graduated from the school in 1891 he composed the song for his class. After vain seeking for something better, he accepted a position as elevator boy, working for $4 a week. In 1893, at the World's Columbian Exposition in Chicago, he was given a position by Frederick Douglass, who was in charge of the exhibit from Hayti. Gradually, with the assistance of friends, chief among whom was Dr. H. A. Tobey, of Toledo, the young poet came into notice as a reader of his verses. *Oak and Ivy* appeared in 1893, and *Majors and Minors* in the winter of 1895-6. William Dean Howells, whose attention had been called to the poet's work, wrote a full-page review of it in the issue of *Harper's Weekly* that contained an account of William McKinley's first nomination for the presidency. Dunbar was now fairly launched upon his larger fame, and *Lyrics of Lowly Life*, published by Dodd, Mead & Co. in 1896, introduced him to the wider reading public. This book is deservedly the poet's best known. It contained the best work of his youth, and was really never surpassed. In 1897 Dunbar enhanced his reputation as a reader of his own poems by a visit to England. About this time he was very busy, writing numerous poems and magazine articles, and meeting with a success that was so much greater than that of most of the versifiers of the day that it became a vogue. In October, 1897, through the influence of Robert G. Ingersoll, he secured employment as an assistant in the Reading Room of the Library of Congress, Washington. He gave up this position after a year however, for the confinement and his late work at night on his own account were making rapid inroads upon his health. On March 6, 1898, Dunbar was married to Alice Ruth Moore, of New Orleans. Early in 1899 he went South, visiting Tuskegee and other schools, and giving many readings. Later in the same year he went to Colorado in a vain search for health. Books were now appearing in rapid succession, short story collections and novels as well as poems. *The Uncalled*, written in London, reflected the poet's thought of entering the ministry. It was followed by *The Love of Landry*, a Colorado story, *The Fanatics*, and *The Sport of the Gods*. Collections of short stories were *Folks from Dixie*, *The Strength of Gideon*, and *In Old Plantation Days*. Volumes of verse were *Lyrics of the Hearthside*, *Lyrics of Love and Laughter*, *Poems of Cabin and Field*, *When Malindy Sings*, *Candle-Lightin' Time*, and *Howdy, Honey, Howdy*, the last four being for the most part profusely illustrated editions of earlier work. The poet's last years were a record of sincere friendships and a losing fight against disease. He died February 9, 1906. He was only thirty-three, but he "had existed millions of years."

Unless the novels are considered as forming a distinct class, Dunbar's work falls naturally into three divisions: the poems in classic English, those in dialect, and the stories in prose. While all his work is remarkably even, it was his verse in the Negro dialect that was his distinct contribution to American literature. That it was not his desire that this should be so may be seen from the eight lines entitled *The Poet*, in which he longed for success in the singing of his "deeper notes" and spoke of his dialect as "a jingle in a broken tongue." Any criticism of Dunbar's English verse will have to reckon with the following poems: *Ere Sleep Comes Down to Soothe the Weary Eyes*, *The Poet and his Song*, *Life*, *Promise and Fulfilment*, *Ships that Pass in the Night*, and *October*. In the pure flow of lyrical verse the poet never surpassed his early lines:

Ere sleep comes down to soothe the weary eyes,
How questioneth the soul that other soul,—
The inner sense which neither cheats nor lies,
But self exposes unto self, a scroll
Full writ with all life's acts unwise or wise,
In characters indelible and known;
So trembling with the shock of sad surprise,
The soul doth view its awful self alone,
Ere sleep comes down to soothe the weary eyes.

Other pieces, no more distinguished in poetic quality, are of special biographical interest. *Robert Gould Shaw* was the expression of pessimism as to the Negro's future in America. *To Louise* was addressed to the young daughter of Dr. Tobey, who, on one occasion when the poet was greatly depressed, in the simple way of a child cheered him by her gift of a rose. *A Death Song* contains the haunting line, "Lay me down beneaf de willers in de grass." *The Monk's Walk* reflects the poet's thought of being a preacher. *To a Violet found on All Saints Day* was the foreboding of domestic unhappiness. Finally there is the swan song contributed to *Lippincott's*—eight exquisite lines:

Because I had loved so deeply,
Because I had loved so long,
God in his great compassion
Gave me the gift of song.

Because I have loved so vainly,
And sung with such faltering breath
The Master in infinite mercy
Offers the boon of Death.

Of the dialect poems by common consent the master-piece is *When Malindy Sings*, a poem inspired by the singing of the poet's mother. Other pieces in dialect that have proved successful are *The Rivals, A Coquette Conquered, The Ol' Tunes, A Corn-Song, When de Co'n Pone's Hot, The Party, Lullaby, At Candle-Lightin' Time, Angelina, Whistling Sam, Two little Boots, The Old Front Gate, To the Eastern Shore,* and *Li'l Gal.* Dunbar was a true poet even if not a great one. His work shows a good sense of form, and at its best is almost poignant in its tenderness.

The short stories of Dunbar are remarkably even in literary merit, and would have been sufficient to make his reputation even if he had not written his poems. One of the best technically is *Jimsella* in the *Folks 'from Dixie* volume. This story exhibits the pathos of the life of unskilled Negroes in the North, and the leading of a little child. *A Family Feud* shows the influence of an old servant in a wealthy Kentucky family. *The Walls of Jericho* is an exposure of the methods of a sensational preacher. *A Supper by Proxy* shows how a Negro's humor may be at hand to save him even when he faces a most desperate situation. Generally these stories attempt no keen satire, simply a faithful portrayal of conditions as they are. Dunbar's novels hardly reach the standard of his best poems and short stories; but *The Sport of the Gods,* by its interesting treatment of a definite phase of life, rises somewhat above the others in strength and workmanship.

By his genius Paul Laurence Dunbar attracted the attention of the great, the wise, and the good. His bookcase contained many autograph copies of the works of distinguished contemporaries. One of the most beautiful pictures in the history of American letters is that of William Dean Howells climbing on one occasion to the top of a cheap apartment house in New York to visit the poet when he was sick. The similarity of the position of Dunbar in American literature to that of Robert Burns in English has frequently been pointed out. In our own time he most readily invites comparison with James Whitcomb Riley. The writings of both men are distinguished by infinite tenderness and pathos; and it is pleasant to know that even before Dunbar published his first book, Riley, already successful, perceived his merit and wrote him a word of cheer.

154. Charles Waddell Chesnutt.—Charles Waddell Chesnutt, the foremost novelist and short story writer of the race, was born in Cleveland, Ohio, June 20, 1858. At the age of sixteen he began to teach in the public schools of North Carolina, from which state his parents had gone to Cleveland; and at the age of twenty-three he became principal of the State Normal

School at Fayetteville. In 1883 he left the South, engaging for a short while in newspaper work in New York City, but going soon to Cleveland, where he worked as a stenographer. He was admitted to the bar in 1887.

While in North Carolina Mr. Chesnutt studied to good purpose the dialect, manners, and superstitions of the Negro people of the State. In 1887 he began in *The Atlantic Monthly* the series of stories which were afterwards brought together in the volume entitled *The Conjure Woman*. This book was published by Houghton, Mifflin & Co., the firm which published also Mr. Chesnutt's other collection of stories and the first two of the three novels which he has written. *The Wife of his Youth, and Other Stories of the Color Line* appeared in 1899. In the same year appeared a compact biography of Frederick Douglass, a contribution to the series of Beacon Biographies of Eminent Americans. Three novels have since appeared, as follows: *The House behind the Cedars*, in 1900; *The Marrow of Tradition*, in 1901; and *The Colonel's Dream*, in 1905.

Mr. Chesnutt's short stories are not all of the same degree of excellence, but the best ones show that he possesses mastery of the short story as a literary form, an art the requisites of which are completely uncomprehended by many of the younger aspirants for literary fame. One of the very best technically is *The*

Bouquet. Most famous of all, however, is *The Wife of his Youth*, a simple work of art whose intensity is almost overpowering. Such stories as these, each setting forth a certain problem, working it out to its logical conclusion, excluding extraneous matter, and, as in *The Bouquet*, selecting the title from the concrete means used in working out the theme, reflect great credit upon the literary skill of the writer.

Of the novels *The House behind the Cedars* is commonly given first place. In the story of the heroine, Rena Walden, are treated some of the most subtle and piercing questions raised by the color-line. *The Marrow of Tradition* touches upon almost every phase of the race problem. *The Colonel's Dream* is a sad story of the failure of high ideals. Colonel Henry French is a man who, born in the South, achieves success in New York and returns to his old home for a little vacation only to find himself face to face with all the problems that one meets in a backward Southern town. He has a dream of " a regenerated South, filled with thriving industries, and thronged with a prosperous and happy people "; but, becoming interested in the justice visited upon the Negroes in the courts and in the employment of white children in the cotton-mills, he encounters opposition to his benevolent plans, and finally goes back to New York defeated. Mr. Chesnutt writes in simple, clear

English, and works with a high sense of art. He is to-day one of the outstanding men of the race in literary achievement, and he deserves credit as a pioneer in treating in the guise of fiction the searching problems that one now meets in the life of the Negro of the South.

155. W. E. Burghardt DuBois.—Aside from his more technical studies Dr. DuBois has produced three books which call for consideration in a review of Negro literature. Of these one is a biography, one a novel, and the other a collection of essays. In 1909 appeared *John Brown*, a contribution to the series of American Crisis Biographies. The subject was one well adapted to treatment at the hands of Dr. DuBois, and in the last chapter, " The Legacy of John Brown," he has shown that his hero has a message for twentieth century America, this: " The cost of liberty is less than the price of repression." The most recent sustained work is *The Quest of the Silver Fleece*, which appeared in 1911. This story has three main themes the economic position of the Negro agricultural laborer, the subsidizing of a certain kind of Negro schools, and Negro life and society in the city of Washington. The third book really appeared before either of the two works just mentioned. In 1903 fourteen essays, most of which had already appeared in such magazines as *The Atlantic Monthly* and *The World's Work*, were brought together in a volume entitled *The Souls of Black Folk*. The remarkable style of this book has made it unquestionably the most important work in classic English yet written by a Negro. It is marked by all the arts of rhetoric, especially by liquid and alliterative effects, strong antithesis, frequent allusion, and poetic suggestiveness. The color-line is " The Veil," the Negro melodies the " Sorrow Songs." Where merit is so even and the standard of performance so high, one hesitates to choose that which is best. *The Dawn of Freedom* is a study of the Freedmen's Bureau ; *The Meaning of Progress* is a story of life in Tennessee told with infinite pathos by one who has been the country school-master ; *The Training of Black Men* is a plea for liberally educated leadership ; *The Quest of the Golden Fleece*, like one or two related essays, is a faithful portrayal of life in the Black Belt ; and *The Coming of John* is the story of what passes in more than one noble soul that has caught a glimpse of the light. The book as a whole is a powerful plea for justice and the liberty of citizenship.

156. William Stanley Braithwaite.—Foremost of the poets of the race at present is William Stanley Braithwaite, of Cambridge, Mass. Mr. Braithwaite has worked for years at his art most conscientiously, and he has taken the time and the pains to master the details and to secure the general equipment that

others all too often deem unimportant. He has published two small books of poems, *Lyrics of Life and
Love* and *The House of Falling Leaves*. His work has
appeared in the *Atlantic*, the *Century*, and other magazines of the first rank; and he is fully abreast with all
recent schools and tendencies. Within the last few
years Mr. Braithwaite s reputation as a critic has even
surpassed his earlier reputation as a writer of verse.
He has encouraged many other workers in literary
fields, and it is not too much to say that he is to-day
the foremost sponsor for current American poetry.
This high position he has won by the articles which
he has written for the Boston *Evening Transcript* and
by the anthology of American magazine poetry that
he has edited for each year since 1913. He has also
edited other anthologies, notably *The Book of Elizabethan Verse*, *The Book of Restoration Verse*, *The Book
of Georgian Verse*, and *Victory*. His position is one of
unique distinction.

157. Other Writers.—In addition to those who have
been mentioned, there have been scores of writers
who would have to be considered in an exhaustive
discussion of Negro literature. Most that has been
written, however, belongs to the field of discussions
of the Negro Problem rather than to that of polite
literature. Many collections of sermons and addresses
have been published; but in the field of theology in

which so much has been attempted no member of the race has yet produced a work that can command the attention of the scholarship of the world, no work, for instance, of the order of Renan's *Life of Jesus* or Strong's *Systematic Theology*. *The History of the Negro Race in America*, by George W. Williams, was a strong contribution to American historical study. This work was the exploration of a new field; and although it is now more than twenty-five years old and not altogether free from errors, it is still too important to be neglected by any student of Negro history. In technical scholarship one is quickly reminded of the work of President William S. Scarborough of Wilberforce, who has published among other things, " First Lessons in Greek " and a treatise on the " Birds " of Aristophanes.

In recent years there have been published a great many works, generally illustrated, on the progress and achievements of the race. A few of these books have been scholarly and serviceable, more have been indifferent, and still more have been worthless. The common fault has been a lack of literary form. Some collaborations, however, have been of more than usual merit. Three may be observed. One is a volume entitled " The Negro Problem," published in 1903 by James Pott & Co., of New York. This consists of seven papers by representative Negroes. Another

collaboration is " From Servitude to Service," published in 1905 by the American Unitarian Association
of Boston. This is made up of the Old South Lectures
on the history and work of Southern institutions for
the education of the Negro. The third book is of
special importance for students of the economic situation of the Negro in the South. It is made up of four
papers, two by Dr. Washington and two by Dr.
DuBois, which were the William Levi Bull Lectures in
the Philadelphia Divinity School for the year 1907.
It is entitled " The Negro in the South," and was
published in 1907 by George W. Jacobs & Co., of
Philadelphia.

Prof. Kelly Miller, of Howard University, and Mr.
Archibald H. Grimké, of Boston, deserve special mention for their strong magazine articles. Professor
Miller has collected some of his very cogent papers
in two volumes, *Race Adjustment* and *Out of the House
of Bondage*, and he has also written an *Appeal to Conscience*. Mr. Grimké has written the lives of Garrison
and Sumner in the American Reformers series. The
work of these two writers, however, belongs rather
to the field of history or sociology than to that of
general literature. To the same province also belongs
William A. Sinclair's *The Aftermath of Slavery*.

In sustained poetic flight and in the classic drama
no member of the race has as yet achieved ultimate

success. In closely related fields, however, an excellent beginning has been made. James W. Johnson has had poems in the *Century* and other prominent magazines, and he has brought together some of his work in *Fifty Years and Other Poems*. Mrs. Georgia Douglas Johnson's *The Heart of a Woman* is representative of recent and promising things in this field. The work of George Moses Horton, whose *Hope of Liberty* appeared in 1829; of Mrs. F. E. W. Harper, whose *Poems on Miscellaneous Subjects* sold thousands of copies soon after the Civil War; and of Albery A. Whitman, who had some of the genuine marks of a poet and who attempted several ambitious productions, all now possesses an interest mainly historical. It is very interesting, however, and is treated at some length in the author's *The Negro in Literature and Art*.

Several persons have written autobiographies. That of Frederick Douglass under several different titles ran through numerous editions. John Mercer Langston's *From the Virginia Plantation to the National Capitol* is interesting and serviceable. The incomparable work in this class of writing, however, is *Up from Slavery*, by Booker T. Washington. The modesty and simplicity of style that characterize this book have made it a model of personal writing. Dr. Washington also produced several other notable books, such as *The Story of the Negro, The Man Far-thest Down*, and *My Larger Education*. The interesting *Autobiography of an Ex-Colored Man* seems to be half fact and half fiction. It was published anonymously, but is generally credited to James W. Johnson.

Numerous attempts at the composition of novels have been made, but it is in this special department that a sense of literary form has been most lacking. With the exception of DuBois's *The Quest of the Silver Fleece*, no work in the field has attracted general attention within the last few years. A. O. Stafford, of Washington, however, has published through the American Book Company a small and very good supplementary reader entitled *Animal Fables 'from the Dark Continent.*

158. The Stage.—In no other field have Negroes with artistic aspirations found the road so hard as it is in that of the legitimate drama. The one or two who have succeeded in this special line have done so only by reason of great individual force, and at the expense of leaving their home country and seeking recognition abroad where their racial affinity would not always debar them.

Conspicuous on the roll of those who have thus triumphed is the name of Ira Frederick Aldridge. About the early life of this man there are conflicting accounts. One says that he was born in Bel Air in

Maryland about 1810, became apprenticed to a German ship carpenter, accompanied Edmund Kean to England as his servant, returning to America about 1830; and another story, not quite so well founded, says that he was the son of a native of Senegal who was brought as a slave to America, that he was born in New York in 1807, and that he was sent to the University of Glasgow to be educated for the ministry. In any case, when he appeared in London in the early thirties, he became a remarkably popular actor. His name always calls up the part of Othello; but he achieved distinction also in other rôles adapted to his color. On the continent of Europe he became regarded as one of the greatest tragedians of the day. He received many decorations of crosses and medals, and became a member of several of the great continental academies of arts and science. The emperors of Russia and Austria and the King of Prussia were among those who honored him. He died in Poland in 1867.

In the closing years of the last century, as the Negro was practically excluded from participation in the regular drama, there came into existence several musical comedy companies whose chief aim was naturally merely to amuse. Out of all such work Bert A. Williams rose to special individual distinction, so that at the present time he is by many critics considered the foremost comedian on the American stage. The last decade is noteworthy both for a beginning in the serious portrayal of Negro life in the general American drama and for the cultivation of the regular drama by the Negro people themselves. The first tendency is represented by Ridgely Torrence's *Granny Maumee* and the second by the work of the Lafayette Players in New York. Both tendencies suggest the possibility of great good in the future.

159. Orators.—In the history of the orators of the race the names of Frederick Douglass, J. C. Price, and Booker T. Washington are conspicuous. Price was for years president of Livingstone College in North Carolina, and his name seems to have become a synonym for eloquence. The speeches of the other two men have become simply a part of the life of the American nation. The real work of the life of Douglass was done before and immediately after the Civil War. Mr. Chesnutt has admirably summed up the characteristics of his oratory. He tells us that " Douglass possessed, in large measure, the physical equipment most impressive in an orator. He was a man of magnificent figure, tall, strong, his head crowned with a mass of hair which made a striking element of his appearance. He had deep-set and flashing eyes, a firm, well-moulded chin, a countenance somewhat severe in repose, but capable of a wide range of expression.

His voice was rich and melodious, and of carrying power." Dr. Booker T. Washington is by general consent one of the first, perhaps the very first, of contemporary American orators. Three of his most notable speeches were delivered in the earlier years of his national prominence. His speech at the Atlanta Exposition of 1895 is famous for its illustration of two ships at sea with the moral, " Cast down your buckets where you are," and for the so-called compromise with the white South : " In all things that are purely social we can be as separate as the fingers, yet one as the hand in all things essential to mutual progress." Shortly after receiving the honorary degree of Master of Arts at the Harvard commencement of 1896, Mr. Washington made a speech in which he emphasized the fact that the welfare of the wealthiest and most cultured person in New England is bound up with that of the humblest man in Alabama, and that each man is his brother's keeper. At the Chicago Peace Jubilee of 1898 he reviewed the conduct of the Negro in the wars of the United States, making a powerful plea for justice to a race which had always chosen the better part in the wars of its country. Mr. Washington has delivered hundreds of addresses, but he has really never surpassed the feeling and point and frankness of these early speeches.

160. Painters.—E. M. Bannister, whose home was

at Providence while he lived, while not known to the younger generation, was very prominent in his art thirty years ago. He gathered about himself a coterie of artists and rich men that formed the nucleus of the Rhode Island Art Club, and one of his pictures took a medal at the Centennial Exposition of 1876.

Incomparably the foremost Negro American painter of the present day is Henry Ossawa Tanner, who was born in Pittsburg June 21, 1859, the son of Bishop Tanner, of the A. M. E. Church. His parents removed to Philadelphia soon after his birth, and there he studied in the public schools and under Thomas Eakins at the Pennsylvania Academy of Fine Arts. In 1882 in Paris he began to study under Jean Paul Laurens, being less conscious of prejudice abroad than at home. He gave some attention to landscape, but soon began to devote himself to scriptural subjects; and it is his religious work which has made him famous. He won honorable mention at the Paris Salon of 1896, a third class medal the next year, a second class medal in 1907, and a medal at the Paris Exposition of 1900. In the United States he was awarded the Walter Lippincott prize in Philadelphia in 1900, and silver medals at Buffalo in 1901, and at St. Louis in 1904. In 1906 he won the Harris prize of $500 for the best picture in the annual exhibition of American paintings at the Chicago Art Institute. *Daniel in the*

Lions' Den, hung in the Salon in 1896, was the first of the line of religious paintings, and *The Raising of Lazarus*, produced in 1897 and bought by the French Government, won for the artist fame. Other prominent titles are *The Annunciation, Christ and Nicodemus, The Two Disciples at the Tomb*, and *The Betrayal*. Within recent years Mr. Tanner has kept pace with some of the newer schools by brilliant experimentation in color and composition. He is thoroughly romantic in tone, and in spirit, if not in technique, there is much to connect him with the Pre-Raphaelites. His whole career is an inspiration and a challenge to younger workers.

William E. Scott, of Indianapolis, is becoming more and more distinguished in mural work, landscape, and portraiture, and among all the painters of the race now working in this country is outstanding. He has spent several years in Paris, and in 1912 and 1913 exhibited pictures in the Salon. He has done much mural work in schools and other public buildings. Some of his effects in coloring are very striking, and in several of his recent pictures he has used racial subjects.

161. Sculptors.— In sculpture several women have risen to recognized position, though, interestingly enough, no man has as yet risen to distinction in this field. Edmonia Lewis, born in New York, first attracted general attention in 1865 by a bust of Robert

Gould Shaw exhibited in Boston. She afterwards made her home in Rome, where she produced *The Freedwoman*, *The Death of Cleopatra*, several busts, and numerous other works of merit. Within the last few decades the work of Mrs. May Howard Jackson, of Washington, has also attracted the attention of the discerning. That of Mrs. Meta Warrick Fuller is now a part of the general story of American sculpture.

Meta Vaux Warrick (now the wife of Dr. S. C. Fuller, of Framingham, Mass.) first compelled serious recognition of her talent by her work in the Pennsylvania School of Industrial Art. Her first original piece in clay was a head of Medusa. This conception, with its hanging jaw, beads of gore on the face, and eyes starting from their sockets, marked her as a sculptor of the horrible. A little later came a crucifix upon which hung a form of Christ torn by anguish. In 1899 the young student went to Paris, where her work brought her in contact with St. Gaudens and other artists. Then there came a day when the great Rodin himself, thrilled by the figure in Secret Sorrow, a man represented as eating his heart out, in the attitude of a father beamed upon the girl and said, " My child, you *are* a sculptor; you have the sense of form." A group entitled *The Wretched* is generally regarded as the artist's masterpiece. Several other early productions were in similar strong and romantic vein; but in recent years Mrs. Fuller has given her attention primarily to themes of social interest, such as freedom, immigration, and peace. A disastrous fire in 1910 destroyed much of her best work, but by 1914 she had recovered sufficiently to be able to hold a public exhibition of her work. *Peace Halting the Ruthlessness of War* in 1917 took the second prize in a competition under the auspices of the Massachusetts Branch of the Woman's Peace Party. Mrs. Fuller leads a busy life, one happy with the virtues of the home, from whose pressing duties she snatches the brief but precious moments for the practice of her art.

162. Vocalists.—It is but natural that soprano singers should have been those most distinguished. Even before the Civil War the Negro race produced one of the first rank in the person of Elizabeth Taylor Greenfield, the " Black Swan," who came into prominence in 1851. This artist, born in Mississippi, was taken to Philadelphia and there cared for by a Quaker lady. Said the *Daily State Register*, of Albany, after one of her concerts: " The compass of her marvelous voice embraces twenty-seven notes, reaching from the sonorous bass of a baritone to a few notes above even Jenny Lind's highest." A voice with a range of more than three octaves naturally attracted much attention in England as well as in America, and comparisons with Jenny Lind, then at the height of her fame, were frequent. Some years later rose Madame Selika, a singer of most uncommon ability and power who won great success on the continent of Europe as well as in America and England. The careers of two later singers are so recent as to be still fresh in the public memory; one indeed may still be heard on the stage. It was in 1887 that Flora Batson entered on the period of her greatest fame. The singing of this artist was, at its best, of the sort that sends an audience into the wildest enthusiasm. At one time at a great temperance revival in New York she sang for ninety successive nights with tremendous effect one song, " Six Feet of Earth Make Us All One Size." Her voice exhibited a compass of three octaves, from the purest, clearcut soprano, sweet and full, to the rich, round notes of the baritone register. Three or four years later than Flora Batson in point both of birth and the period of greatest artistic success came Mrs. Sissieretta Jones, with whose name the " S'wanee River " is almost inseparably linked in the public mind. Her voice is of great volume and unusual richness; it exhibits also the peculiar plaintive quality ever characteristic of the Negro voice.

Within the last few years among the very prominent singers have been Mme. E. Azalia Hackley, Mme. Anita Patti Brown, Mme. Mayme Calloway Byron, and Mme. Florence Cole-Talbert. Mme. Hackley has a splendid musical temperament and has enjoyed the benefit of three years of study in Paris and other European cities. She has assisted many individuals and in other ways done much to show the capabilities of the Negro voice. Mme. Brown, a product of the Chicago conservatories, is the possessor of a voice with a sympathetic quality that makes a ready appeal to the heart of an audience. Mme. Byron has but lately returned to America after years of study and cultivation in Europe. She has sung in the principal theatres abroad and in other ways met with distinguished success. Mme. Talbert has within the last few years sung in the chief cities of the North and West with an increasing measure of success. Of the men Harry T. Burleigh commands instant attention. For more than twenty years he has been the baritone soloist at St. George's Episcopal Church, New York, and for nearly as long at Temple Emanu-El, the Fifth Avenue Jewish synagogue. Roland W. Hayes, a brilliant tenor, has within the last decade filled numerous engagements all over the country with noteworthy success. In addition to those who have been mentioned there are to-day at work several younger singers who need only a little more training and opportunity to secure from the public the high place that they deserve.

163. Fisk Jubilee Singers.—In this general review

of those who have helped to make the Negro voice famous, mention should be made of a remarkable company of singers who first made the folk-songs of the race known to the world at large. In 1871 the Fisk Jubilee Singers began their memorable progress through America and Europe, meeting at first with scorn and sneers, but before long touching the heart of the world with their strange music. The original band consisted of four young men and five young women; in the seven years of the existence of the company altogether twenty-four persons were enrolled in it. Says J. B. Marsh in his little book, *The Story of the Jubilee Singers:* "They were at times without money to buy needed clothing; yet in three years they returned, bringing back with them nearly one hundred thousand dollars. They had been turned away from hotels and driven out of railway waiting-rooms, because of their color; but they had been received with honor by the President of the United States; they had sung their slave songs before the Queen of Great Britain, and they had gathered as invited guests about the breakfast table of her Prime Minister. Their success was as remarkable as their mission was unique." Altogether these singers by their seven years of work raised one hundred and fifty thousand dollars, and secured for their institution school books, paintings, and apparatus to the value of seven or eight thousand more. They sang in the United States, England, Scotland, Ireland, Holland, Switzerland, and Germany. Since their time they have been much imitated, but hardly ever equalled, and never surpassed.

164. Composers.—The foremost name on the roll of Negro composers is that of a man whose home was in England, but who in so many ways identified himself with the Negroes in the United States that he deserves to be considered here. Samuel Coleridge-Taylor (1875–1912) was born in London, and began the study of the violin when he was six years old. As he grew older he emphasized more and more the violin and the piano. In 1890 he became a student in the violin department of the Royal Academy of Music. In his third year at this institution he won a prize in composition, and in 1894 was graduated with honor. His early works include a number of anthems and some chamber-music. In 1898 Coleridge-Taylor became famous by his cantata, " Hiawatha's Wedding-Feast." This was followed by " The Death of Minnehaha " and " Hiawatha's Departure." His most distinctive work, however, is that reflecting his interest in the Negro folk-song. "Characteristic of the melancholy beauty, barbaric color, charm of musical rhythm and vehement passion of the true Negro music, are his symphonic pianoforte selections based on the Negro melodies from Africa and

America, the 'African Suite,' a group of pianoforte
pieces, the 'African Romances' (words by Paul L.
Dunbar), the 'Song of Slavery,' 'Three Choral Ballads' and 'African Dances,' and a suite for violin
and pianoforte."* Prominent later vocal works are
" The Atonement " and " The Blind Girl of Castel-
Cuille." This great musician also wrote the music
to " Herod "; " Othello," a suite for pianoforte; " A
Tale of Old Japan," his last choral work, and various
waltzes, as well as other things. All of his works
show breadth of treatment and effects of beauty at-
tained by simple means.

The foremost composer of the race to-day is Harry
T. Burleigh, who within the last few years has won
a place not only among the prominent song-writers
of America, but of the world. His compositions dis-
play great technical excellence. Prominent among
his later songs are *Jean*, the *Saracen Songs, One Year*
(1914–1915), and *The Young Warrior*, the brilliant
war-song the words of which were by James W. Johnson. Of somewhat stronger quality even than most
of these songs are *The Grey Wolf*, to words by Arthur
Symons, *The Soldier*, a setting of Rupert Brooke's
well known sonnet, and *Ethiopia Saluting the Colors*.
An entirely different division of Mr. Burleigh's work,
hardly less important than his songs, is his various

* *Crisis*, Oct. 1912.

adaptations of the Negro melodies, especially for choral work; and he assisted *Dvorak* in his New World Symphony based on the Negro folk-songs. For his general achievement in music he was in 1917 awarded the Spingarn Medal. Another prominent composer is Will Marion Cook. Mr. Cook's time has been given largely to the composition of popular music; he has, however, produced numerous songs that bear the stamp of genius. In 1912 a group of his tuneful and characteristic pieces was published by Schirmer. J. Rosamond Johnson is also a composer with many original ideas. In pure melody he is not surpassed by any other musician of the race to-day. His long experience with large orchestras, moreover, has given him unusual knowledge of instrumentation. Carl Diton, organist and pianist, has so far been interested chiefly in the transcription for the organ of representative Negro melodies. R. Nathaniel Dett has the merit, more than others, of attempting works in large form. Of the very young men of promise, special interest attaches to the work of Edmund T. Jenkins, of Charleston, S. C., who a few years ago made his way to the Royal Academy in London, and who in the course of his career at this institution has already taken numerous prizes, in composition as well as for instrumental work.

165. Other Musicians.—Raymond Augustus Law-

son, of Hartford, Conn., is probably the foremost
pianist of the race. His technique is most highly
developed, and his style causes him to be a favorite
concert pianist. He conducts one of the leading
studios in New England and enjoys a wealthy cli-
entele. While he and J. Rosamond Johnson and Roy
W. Tibbs and Hazel Harrison cannot possibly be
overlooked, there are to-day so many excellent pianists
that a most competent and well-informed musician
would hesitate before passing judgment upon them.
Of the organists Melville Charlton, of Brooklyn, is
prominent. As an associate of the American Guild
of Organists he has now won for himself a place among
the foremost organists of the United States, and as he
is still a young man, from him may not unreasonably
be expected many years of high artistic endeavor.
Two other organists who have for years been very
prominent are William Herbert Bush, of New London,
Conn., and Frederick P. White, of Boston. Prominent violinists within recent years have been Clarence
Cameron White, of Boston, Joseph Douglass, of
Washington, Felix Weir, of Washington and New
York, and Kemper Harreld, of Chicago and Atlanta.
" Blind Tom " (Thomas Bethune, born in Columbus,
Ga., in 1849), who attracted so much attention in
the earlier years after the Civil War, deserves notice
as a prodigy rather than as a musician of solid

achievement. He was peculiarly susceptible to the influences of nature, imitated on the piano all the sounds he knew, and without being able to read a note could play from memory the most difficult compositions of Beethoven and Mendelssohn.

BIBLIOGRAPHY

The following compilation is by no means full even for the present work. It seeks merely to mention by way of acknowledgment the books which have been of most service and which are cited in the footnotes. The special student will of course consult the "Select List of References on the Negro Question," published by the Government, Washington, 1906, or, better still, "A Select Bibliography of the Negro American," edited by Dr. W. E. B. DuBois, Atlanta, 1905. Even these works will have to be supplemented for the last twelve years. The attention of those who might be specially interested in the artistic life of the Negro is invited to the bibliography in the present author's "The Negro in Literature and Art" (Duffield, New York, 1918). Dr. Carter G. Woodson's "The Education of the Negro Prior to 1861" (Putnam's, New York, 1915) contains an excellent special bibliography, and the *Journal of Negro History* is constantly suggestive of good material.

COLLECTIONS OR SERIES

Atlanta University Studies of Negro Problems, especially No. 8, The Negro Church, No. 12, Economic Co-operation among Negro Americans, and No. 15, The College-Bred Negro American.

Johns Hopkins University Studies in Historical and Political Science (special numbers cited below).

Occasional Papers of the American Negro Academy, especially No. 7, Right on the Scaffold, or the Martyrs of 1822, by A. H. Grimké, and No. 11, The Negro and the Elective Franchise.

Journal of Negro History, 1916–. Washington, D.C.

Publications of the United States Bureau of Education: Chapters from the Report of the Commissioner of Education; For 1900–1901, Chapter XVI, The Education of the Negro, and Chapter XX, The Public School Problem of the South; for 1904, Chapter VI, The Work and Influence of Hampton; for 1908, Chapter XXII, Schools for the Colored Race.

Bulletin 129, "Negroes in the United States," from Census of 1910. Washington, 1915.

Annual reports of General Education Board, and other boards interested in the education of the Negro.

Bureau of Education, Bulletin, 1916, No. 39. Negro Education, a Study of the Private and Higher Schools for Colored People in the United States, by Thomas Jesse Jones. Washington, 1917.

The Pro-Slavery Argument (as maintained by the most distinguished writers of the Southern states). Charleston, 1852.

Statutes at Large, being a collection of all the Laws of Virginia from the first session of the Legislature, in the year 1619, by William Waller Hening. Richmond, 1819–20.

The Statutes at Large of South Carolina, edited by Thomas Cooper. Columbia, S. C., 1837.

Laws of the State of North Carolina, compiled by Henry Potter, J. L. Taylor, and Bart. Yancey. Raleigh, 1821.

INDIVIDUAL WORKS

William T. Alexander: *History of the Colored Race in America.* Palmetto Publishing Co., New Orleans, 1887.

Ray Stannard Baker: *Following the Colour Line.* Doubleday, Page & Co., New York, 1908.

James Curtis Ballagh: *White Servitude in the Colony of Virginia,* Nos. VI–VII of Series XIII of Johns Hopkins Studies. The Johns Hopkins Press, Baltimore, 1895.

A History of Slavery in Virginia, extra volume XXIV in Johns Hopkins Studies. The Johns Hopkins Press, Baltimore, 1902.

John Spencer Bassett: *Slavery and Servitude in the Colony of*

North Carolina, Nos. IV–V of Series XIV of Johns Hopkins Studies. The Johns Hopkins Press, Baltimore, 1896.

Anti-Slavery Leaders of North Carolina, No. VI of Series XVI of Johns Hopkins Studies. The Johns Hopkins Press, Baltimore, 1898.

W. O. Blake: *The History of Slavery and the Slave-Trade.* Columbus, O., 1861.

William Stanley Braithwaite: *The House of Falling Leaves* (Poems). J. W. Luce & Co., Boston, 1908.

Lyrics of Life and Love (Poems). H. B. Turner & Co., Boston, 1904.

The Book of Elizabethan Verse (Anthology). H. B. Turner & Co., Boston, 1906.

The Book of Georgian Verse (Anthology). Brentano's, New York, 1909.

The Book of Restoration Verse (Anthology). Brentano's, New York, 1910.

Anthology of Magazine Verse for each year since 1913 (early volumes originally issued by different publishers, but all now regularly handled and the later ones issued by Small, Maynard & Co., Boston).

The Poetic Year (for 1916): A Critical Anthology. Small, Maynard & Co., Boston, 1917.

The Golden Treasury of Magazine Verse. (Anthology.) Small, Maynard & Co., Boston, 1918.

Victory: Celebrated by Thirty-eight American Poets (Anthology). Small, Maynard & Co., Boston, 1919.

Benjamin Brawley: *A Short History of the American Negro.* The Macmillan Co., New York (originally issued 1913).

History of Morehouse College. Published by the College, Atlanta, 1917.

The Negro in Literature and Art. Duffield & Co., New York, 1918.

Your Negro Neighbor (in Our National Problems series). The Macmillan Co., New York, 1918.

New Era Declamations (edited). The University Press, Sewanee, Tenn., 1918.

Africa and the War. Duffield & Co., New York, 1918.

Women of Achievement (specially written for the Fireside Schools under the auspices of the Woman's American Baptist Home Mission Society). Chicago, 1919.

Edward MacKnight Brawley: *The Negro Baptist Pulpit,* American Baptist Publication Society, Philadelphia, 1890.

Walter H. Brooks: *The Silver Bluff Church.* Washington, 1910.

Andrew Carnegie: *The Negro in America.* The Committee of Twelve, Cheyney, Pa.

Charles Waddell Chesnutt: *Frederick Douglass, A Biography.* Small, Maynard & Co., Boston, 1899.

The Conjure Woman (Stories). Houghton Mifflin Co., Boston, 1899.

The Wife of his Youth, and Other Stories of the Color Line. Houghton Mifflin Co., Boston, 1899.

The House Behind the Cedars (Novel). Houghton Mifflin Co., Boston, 1900.

The Marrow of Tradition (Novel). Houghton Mifflin Co., Boston, 1901.

The Colonel's Dream (Novel). Doubleday, Page & Co., New York, 1905.

John R. Commons: *Races and Immigrants in America.* The Macmillan Co., New York, 1907.

John W. Cromwell: *The Negro in American History.* The American Negro Academy, Washington, 1914.

William Edward Burghardt DuBois: *Suppression of the African Slave-Trade.* Longmans, Green & Co., New York, 1896 (now handled through Harvard University Press, Cambridge).

The Philadelphia Negro. University of Pennsylvania, Philadelphia, 1899.

The Souls of Black Folk. Essays and Sketches. A. C. McClurg & Co., Chicago, 1903.

The Negro in the South (with Booker T. Washington). George W. Jacobs & Co., Philadelphia, 1907.

John Brown (in American Crisis Biographies). George W. Jacobs & Co., Philadelphia, 1909.

The Quest of the Silver Fleece (Novel).   A. C. McClurg & Co., Chicago, 1911.

The Negro (in Home University Library series).   Henry Holt & Co., New York, 1915.

(See also Atlanta University Publications.)

Paul Laurence Dunbar: Life and Works, edited by Lida Keck Wiggins.   J. L. Nichols & Co., Naperville, Ill., 1907.

(All of Dunbar's work, except the musical sketch, is published by Dodd, Mead & Co., New York.)

POEMS:—

Lyrics of Lowly Life, 1896.

Lyrics of the Hearthside, 1899.

Lyrics of Love and Laughter, 1903.

Lyrics of Sunshine and Shadow, 1905.

Complete Poems, 1913.

SPECIALLY ILLUSTRATED VOLUMES OF POEMS:—

Poems of Cabin and Field, 1899.

Candle-Lightin' Time, 1901.

When Malindy Sings, 1903.

Li'l' Gal, 1904.

Howdy, Honey, Howdy, 1905.

Joggin' Erlong, 1906.

Speakin' o' Christmas, 1914.

NOVELS:—

The Uncalled, 1898.

The Love of Landry, 1900.

The Fanatics, 1901.

The Sport of the Gods, 1902.

STORIES AND SKETCHES:—

Folks from Dixie, 1898.

The Strength of Gideon, and Other Stories, 1900.

In Old Plantation Days, 1903.

The Heart of Happy Hollow, 1904.

Uncle Eph's Christmas, a one-act musical sketch.   Washington, 1900.

Hamilton James Eckenrode: *The Political History of Virginia during the Reconstruction*, Nos. 6, 7, 8 of Series XXII of

Johns Hopkins Studies. The Johns Hopkins Press, Baltimore, 1904.

George W. Ellis: *Negro Culture in West Africa.* The Neale Publishing Co., New York, 1914.

Abraham Epstein: *The Negro Migrant in Pittsburgh* (in publications of the School of Economics of the University of Pittsburgh), 1918.

Albert Bernhardt Faust: *The German Element in the United States.* Houghton Mifflin Co., Boston, 1909.

Thomas P. Fenner: *Religious Folk-Songs of the Negro* (new edition). The Institute Press, Hampton, Va., 1909.

Walter L. Fleming: *Documentary History of Reconstruction.* The Arthur H. Clark Co., Cleveland, 1907.

Archibald H. Grimké: *Right on the Scaffold, or the Martyrs of 1822.* No. 7 of the Papers of the American Negro Academy, Washington.

Albert Bushnell Hart: *Negro Suffrage*, a contribution to the Boston *Transcript* of March 24, 1906, reprinted as a pamphlet by the Niagara Movement.

George Edmund Haynes: *The Negro at Work in New York City* (in Columbia University Studies in History, Economics and Public Law). 1912.

Hinton Rowan Helper: *The Impending Crisis of the South: How to Meet It.* A. B. Burdick, New York, 1857.

Georgia Douglas Johnson: *The Heart of a Woman, and Other Poems.* The Cornhill Co., Boston, 1917.

James W. Johnson: *Autobiography of an Ex-Colored Man* (published anonymously). Sherman, French & Co., Boston, 1912.

Fifty Years and Other Poems. The Cornhill Co., Boston, 1917.

Henry E. Krehbiel: *Afro-American Folk-Songs.* G. Schirmer, New York and London, 1914.

John R. Lynch: *The Facts of Reconstruction.* The Neale Publishing Co., New York, 1913.

George S. Merriam: *The Negro and the Nation.* Henry Holt & Co., New York, 1906.

Kelly Miller: *Race Adjustment.* The Neale Publishing Co., New York and Washington, 1908.
Out of the House of Bondage. The Neale Publishing Co., New York, 1914.
Appeal to Conscience (in Our National Problems series). The Macmillan Co., New York, 1918.
(See also Chapter XVI, *The Education of the Negro*, in Report of the United States Commissioner in Education for 1900–1901.)
Freeman Henry Morris Murray: *Emancipation and the Freed in American Sculpture.*
Frederick Law Olmstead: *Journey in the Seaboard Slave States.* New York, 1856.
The Cotton Kingdom. New York, 1861.
James Ford Rhodes: *History of the United States 1850–1877.* The Macmillan Co., New York, 1906.
W. C. Berwick Sayers: *Samuel Coleridge-Taylor: Musician; His Life and Letters.* Cassell & Co., London and New York, 1915.
Emmett J. Scott and Lyman Beecher Stowe: *Booker T. Washington, Builder of a Civilization.* Doubleday, Page & Co., Garden City, N. Y., 1916.
L. A. Scruggs: *Women of Distinction.* Raleigh, N. C., 1893.
Wilbur H. Siebert: *The Underground Railroad from Slavery to Freedom.* The Macmillan Co., New York, 1898.
James M. Simms: *The First Colored Baptist Church in North America.* Printed by J. B. Lippincott Co., Philadelphia, 1888.
J. G. Steward: *The Haitian Revolution 1791 to 1804.* Thomas Y. Crowell Co., New York, 1914.
Alfred Holt Stone: "The Negro in the South" (article in Volume X of *The South in the Building of the Nation*). The Southern Historical Publication Society, Richmond, 1909.
James M. Trotter: *Music and Some Highly Musical People.* Boston, 1878.
Booker T. Washington: *The Future of the American Negro.* Small, Maynard & Co., Boston, 1899.

The Story of my Life and Work.   Nichols & Co., Naperville, Ill., 1900.

Up from Slavery. An Autobiography.   Doubleday, Page & Co., New York, 1901.

Character Building.   Doubleday, Page & Co., New York, 1902.

Working with the Hands.   Doubleday, Page & Co., New York, 1904.

Putting the Most into Life.   Crowell & Co., New York, 1906.

Frederick Douglass (in American Crisis Biographies).   George W. Jacobs & Co., Philadelphia, 1906.

The Negro in the South (with W. E. B. DuBois).   George W. Jacobs & Co., Philadelphia, 1907.

The Negro in Business.   Hertel, Jenkins & Co., Chicago, 1907.

The Story of the Negro.   Doubleday, Page & Co., New York, 1909.

My Larger Education.   Doubleday, Page & Co., Garden City, N. Y., 1911.

The Man Farthest Down (with Robert Emory Park).   Doubleday, Page & Co., Garden City, N. Y., 1912.

Phillis Wheatley: *Letters,* edited by C. Deane, privately printed, Boston, 1864.

Poems on Various Subjects, London, 1773.   (This is the rare first edition.   The latest and most accessible reprint is that published by the A. M. E. Book Concern, Philadelphia, 1909.)

George W. Williams: *History of the Negro Race in America.*   G. P. Putnam's Sons, New York and London, 1883.

Carter G. Woodson: *The Education of the Negro Prior to 1861.*   G. P. Putnam's Sons, New York and London, 1915.

A Century of Negro Migration.   G. P. Putnam's Sons, New York and London, 1918.

Richard Robert Wright: *Negro Companies of the Spanish Explorers.*   (Pamphlet reprinted from the *American Anthropologist,* Vol. 4, April–June, 1902.)

Richard Robert Wright, Jr.: *Self-Help in Negro Education*   The Committee of Twelve, Cheyney, Pa.

INDEX

www.ingramcontent.com/pod-product-compliance
Lightning Source LLC
Chambersburg PA
CBHW050804270326
41926CB00025B/4528